The Art of
COOKING MORELS

The Art of
COOKING MORELS

Ruth Mossok Johnston

ILLUSTRATIONS BY David McCall Johnston

THE UNIVERSITY OF MICHIGAN PRESS | Ann Arbor

Published in the United States of America by
The University of Michigan Press
Manufactured in China
♾ Printed on acid-free paper

2015   2014   2013   2012   4   3   2   1

A CIP catalog record for this book is available from
the British Library.

Library of Congress Cataloging-in-Publication Data

Johnston, Ruth Mossok.
    The art of cooking morels / Ruth Mossok
  Johnston ; illustrations by David McCall
  Johnston.
        p. cm.
    Includes index.
    ISBN 978-0-472-11784-0 (cloth : alk. paper)
    1. Cooking (Morels) 2. Morels. I. Title.
  TX804.J64 2011
  641.6'58—dc23   2011023781

Acknowledgments

Thanks first and foremost to my husband, David McCall Johnston (of more than thirty years), for the faith, support, encouragement, and sheer talent to accompany me on any life's path or project. How blessed I am to have not only found my soul mate and the love of my life, but an equal partner in every aspect of that life. The art that accompanies this journey, *The Art of Cooking Morels,* enhances my book to levels I could never realize without him.

Ellen McCarthy—my editor, and champion of this book at the University of Michigan Press—who saw the vision from the beginning and helped make *The Art of Cooking Morels* an absolute reality. The additional plus—beyond great editing—Ellen has a love of food and an understanding of the prized fungi. Scott Ham for his involvement and contributions, Mary Sexton, University of Michigan Press, for her talent and sensitivity in design, along with the rest of the University of Michigan Press Staff.

Earthy Delights out of DeWitt, Michigan, specifically Ed Baker, without whom I could have not done this book. His provision of morels when I was unable to find them elsewhere, and his continued supply throughout my recipe efforts (fresh and dried), will always be appreciated, almost as much as his true friendship. And Chef David Eger—who was a great contact at Earthy so I didn't have to bother Ed all the time!

My precious and beloved father, Joe Mossok, who forever remains in my heart, as my greatest supporter and cheerleader, and my dear friend Norma Goldman, who has taken up that gauntlet with fervor (and duties as an official taste tester).

Graham Kerr, my dear friend and mentor, the man I grew up watching, along with Julia Child, who fueled my initial passion for cooking and food. I thank him for his friendship, his prayers, and the encouragement he always supplies me with. Chris Hughes, Broken Arrow Ranch out of Ingram, Texas (BAR was a great find by my daughter, Kim), for his gracious supply of wild game while I was developing recipes.

Nordic Ware, Cuisinart, and Microplane Corporations—the special companies that I relied on for great products to use during recipe development.

My children, Jordan and Kim, who are always a constant blessing and source of unconditional love, and are by far my greatest accomplishment! My grandchildren, Octavio and Nolan, who have participated in making dumplings with morels and ramps, listened to parts of the text during our family vacation, and even posed for photos that then became beautiful art.

My treasured friends who have been wonderfully supportive throughout this process (too many to name individually, with the exceptions of Sara Jane Keidan, who ate morels until they were coming out of her ears, and Norma Goldman)—all of those who continually came to taste test recipes, tried making my recipes, and lived these recipes with me as they were produced.

Marsha Kahn Markle who is more a sister than an ex-sister-in-law . . . who was, and is, a constant source of encouragement even though she may be a mere 2,000 miles away.

I thank you.

Contents

APPETIZERS

SOUPS

ENTRÉES

SIDE DISHES

ADDITIONAL TIPS
123

Handling Fresh and Dried Morels
133

Ingredients that Marry Well
with Morels
135

Index of Ingredients
137

I do not claim to be a mycologist or any type of mushroom expert—what I am is passionate about wild mushrooms, specifically morels. It doesn't hurt that I have been a food writer/journalist for more than twenty-five years, taught at a culinary school, and have been a food consultant and Editorial Director for all the books on food, culinary and nutrition for McGraw-Hill—but most of all and paramount in my life, I love to cook, experience, and create food . . . morels are way up there on my passion meter. About fifteen years ago, when interviewed on radio talking about wild mushrooms and asked about finding and picking wild shrooms, my response consisted of a mention "if you don't have a mushroom expert with you, make sure to leave some mushrooms in the fridge for the medical examiner." While this received a great laugh, I reminded the interviewer, I wasn't kidding. Along with credible identification of these prized fungi is the knowledge that you never eat raw wild mushrooms! They must be cooked prior to consumption.

Why this passion? Always adventuresome, always not quite mainstream (in lots of ways)—my food tastes and experiences were fueled throughout my childhood—not guided by parental modeling or instruction, but by parental exposure. My Midwestern, potato chip company owner father who ate nothing but ground sirloin and a plain steak, and my New York, Mahattanite mother who had far more an adventuresome palate, but no particular interest in preparation of anything, including daily meals, knew early on my experience needed to be different. And that, most definitely was provided. They took me for meals everywhere, especially fine dining in New York and any other city we traveled to—they watched as I consumed Peanut Stuffed Lobster at the old Clam Shop in Detroit, as my father gasped in disbelief. But, the point is, they did it. They provided the canvas . . . and how grateful I am to those parents that put me first in so many ways.

As a child I always wanted the "weirdest" thing on the menu—wild boar, absolutely. Wild mushrooms, all the better. Was it always the most expensive? Not necessarily, but sometimes. Key for me, the experience. And, that hasn't changed much today. I still seek out the unusual, and always with the best result—my husband insists I always pick the best thing on the menu, sniff out the most esoteric ingredients, and call it my own (as in adoption), or find the most interesting restaurant by happenstance.

In the 1990s I met Joe Breidenstein from Walloon Lake, Michigan—a bright, tender, and generous man who was passionate about morels. He developed morel week-end outings, simultaneously promoting Michigan, local woodsy finds, and a bevy of mushroom specialists as friends and compadres, I would go up during spring and fall and do mushroom cooking for his guests. Even when I moved to Illinois for five years, Joe continued to use my recipes for his weekends. Joe became a close and treasured friend—a special friendship that lasted until his death in 2009. I loved Joe, I loved his passion, and I loved morels.

And thus, I dedicate this book in his memory with the hope that you will become as passionate about our favorite wild mushroom—the prized morel.

Author's Note

So do we call it a philosophy of cooking? Or just what goes into my thought process and delivery of foods cooked in my professional kitchen and throughout this book . . . geared to making foods delicious and healthy by eliminating as much fat, sugar, and salt as possible, using substitutes and creative alternatives, without diminishing flavor or quality of the final products.

I am not a dietitian or nutritionist, just a passionate food writer and journalist determined to keep the foods I share within a legitimate dietary framework and make them absolutely delicious. No one should walk away feeling they have missed anything! The added bonus of these recipes, a focus on one of my personal favorites— morels.

We all understand that morels pair beautifully with butter and cream; that is a given. Talk to any forager, chef, or promoter of wild mushrooms (especially morels). And, I couldn't agree more . . . if it is done in moderation for most people, it works in helping to keep a healthy diet. But for people like my husband who is a survivor of a heart attack, open heart surgery, diabetes, and cancer, we are talking making foods that are healthy and delicious and making it a life choice.

David's first major medical crisis was in 1987. Here we are in 2011 and he is healthy and, without question, well fed. His doctor applauds his "numbers" and the fact that he has maintained his health through myriad health issues. Much is certainly attributed to the food that is prepared for him and portion control. Yes, David is fortunate to have a wife who writes cookbooks and develops recipes—but anyone can take this book and competently prepare any and all of the recipes included. As I say in all my cookbooks, prepare the recipes as directed, and you will have a successful outcome: add your own creativity, and learn to create. This goes for fats, sweeteners, herbs, spices, grains, vegetables, and proteins.

You will notice throughout, I do use olive oil (usually extra virgin), olive oil spray, and butter substitute. If you aren't concerned about restrictions, make your own decisions and adjustments. For many recipes utilizing sugar, I may use agave nectar, which is lower on the glycemic scale, or turbinado sugar from evaporated cane juice. In that case, obviously, regular sugar will substitute just fine. I also keep the salt low, so adjust to your own tastes and sensibilities.

A Note Regarding Olive Oil Spray

The best olive oil cooking spray is a good quality olive oil put in a small spray bottle made for that purpose. This process is not only less expensive than canned commercial sprays; it also protects nonstick pans from damage and build-up on the surface of the pan's manufactured coating. Where indicated throughout the book, olive oil spray is in fact, good quality olive oil in a specific spray container.

APPETIZERS

David McCall Johnston

Wow your guests with this easy and elegant appetizer of cheese, artichokes, ramps, and morels with a hint of rum . . . add some fruit to accompany the brie en croûte along with biscuits, crackers, or flat bread.

Brie en Croûte with Artichoke, Ramps, and Morels

Directions:
Preheat oven to 350°F. Place oven rack to middle position.

Coat a 9-inch quiche dish with cooking spray and set aside.

Coat a medium-sized sauté pan with cooking spray and sauté morels over medium heat for 6 minutes. Add rum and stir about 2 minutes or until rum is absorbed. Add ramps and cook for an additional 4 minutes or until ramps are lightly brown. Set aside to cool.

In a microwave or on the stove, steam the frozen artichokes until defrosted and lightly warmed. Set aside to cool.

While morels, ramps, and artichoke hearts cool, lay one circle of pastry in the bottom of the prepared quiche dish. Place brie wheel in center of bottom pastry. The wheel should be smaller than the quiche dish, allowing for at least 1 1/2 inches to fill with your mixture.

In a food processor, process the morels, ramps, and artichokes on pulse, only to rough chop (or chop with a knife). Place chopped mixture around the outside of the brie in the pastry (this should fill in the space between the brie and the sides of the dish). Place the remaining pastry circle over the entire top of the dish. Trim away any excess pastry and reserve for a design. Gently pinch together edges all around the circle and lightly crimp to form a nice decorated edge. Make sure pastry is flat on top and contains no air bubbles. Brush top and sides of pastry with beaten egg, and add a cutout decoration to top if desired.

Bake the pastry-covered brie in the preheated oven for 60 minutes, or until pastry is nicely browned.

Yield: 12–16 servings

Ingredients:
Olive oil cooking spray
8 ounces fresh morels, lightly brushed and rinsed
2 (9-inch) pie crusts (homemade or prepared), rolled out and chilled in the refrigerator
1/2 cup sliced ramps (white and light purple parts only)
1/4 cup spiced rum
1 package (12 ounces) frozen artichoke quarters
1 (16-ounce) brie wheel, unwrapped
1 egg, beaten

Special Equipment:
1 fluted 9-inch quiche dish or pie plate
Food processor
Pastry brush

Chicken and Morel Satay with Peanut Sauce

Chicken and morels on a stick with a nut-infused sauce! For a slight flavor change use cashew or almond butter in place of the peanut butter. Use as an appetizer or serve several to each person as an entrée. Serve satay on a retro pupu platter, or serve over a bed of rice or steamed vegetables, for a great presentation.

Yield: 10 skewers

Ingredients for Chicken, Morels, and Marinade:

1 1/2 pounds chicken breast meat, sliced (1/4 of an inch or desired thickness)

20 fresh morels or dried, reconstituted, lightly brushed (if fresh, rinse lightly if necessary and carefully dry), whole

3 tablespoons freshly squeezed lime juice (2 large or 3 small limes)

1 tablespoon freshly grated ginger root or crystallized ginger, minced

2 tablespoons olive oil

2 teaspoons Thai fish sauce (choose lowest-sodium possible)

1 Thai red pepper (or crushed red pepper flakes)

Special Equipment:

10-inch skewers—metal or bamboo (if bamboo, soak overnight prior to use)

Grill

Wire whisk

Directions for Chicken, Morels, and Marinade:

In a glass bowl, add the chicken slices, lime juice, ginger, olive oil, fish sauce, and red pepper; toss lightly, cover with plastic wrap, and refrigerate for 2 hours. *Note:* You may want to make the Peanut Sauce while the chicken is marinating.

Once clean or reconstituted, coat the morels with cooking spray on both sides; set aside.

Remove from fridge and thread chicken on skewers, adding morels between the chicken—2 morels per skewer and 3 pieces of meat (or any configuration, you choose).

When ready to cook, coat grill grate with cooking spray or dampen a paper towel with olive oil and wipe grate. Preheat grill to medium-high. Reduce heat to medium; place skewers on grill and cover the grill. Cook 4–8 minutes (depending on thickness of meat—check after 3 minutes) and turn over to the other side and continue to grill for an additional 4–8 minutes or until chicken has grill marks and appears cooked. *Note:* Keep an eye on the morels—you don't want them to burn!

Directions for Peanut Sauce (makes about 2 cups):

Coat a medium-sized saucepan with olive oil cooking spray and place over medium heat; sauté the onions and garlic over medium-high heat until transparent, 2–3 minutes. Add the chile peppers and continue to sauté for 2 more minutes. Add the ponzu, ginger, anchovy paste, brown sugar, cumin, Chinese five-spice powder, and cardamom; stir until well blended.

Reduce heat to medium-low, and add the coconut milk; mix well. Add the peanut butter and continue to cook over very low heat for 20–22 minutes, stirring occasionally. When mixture appears thick and darkened, remove from the heat and whisk in the half-and-half until well mixed. Add a little water, until the desired consistency is achieved. Serve the sauce at room temperature with the Chicken Satay.

Ingredients for Peanut Sauce:

Olive oil cooking spray

1 medium onion, peeled and finely chopped

2–3 garlic cloves, peeled and minced

2–3 fresh hot green chile peppers (or Thai peppers, deveined and seeds removed), minced

1/2 teaspoon ponzu or light soy sauce with a bit of citrus

1 teaspoon ground ginger

1 teaspoon anchovy paste

2 teaspoons light brown sugar

1 teaspoon ground cumin

1 teaspoon Chinese five-spice powder

1 teaspoon ground cardamom

1/3 cup light coconut milk

1 cup low-fat, low-sodium creamy peanut butter

1 1/2 cups fat-free half-and-half

Water (about 1/4 cup to thin out the sauce to desired consistency)

Note: For those with allergies, this recipe does contain fish.

Deviled Quail Eggs with Morels

Even if you don't like deviled eggs, you will like these! The buttery flavor of the yolk paired with the chopped morels makes for a very special treat: tiny eggs but not tiny in flavor or presentation. Ideas: place a drop of the filling on a small scallop shell and yolk "glue" a deviled quail egg for serving; set one on a small square cracker as a one-bite delight, or place one on an Asian spoon for serving. Presentation can be so powerful with this appetizer—so many possibilities!

Yield: 80 deviled quail eggs (halves)

Ingredients:

40 fresh quail eggs
1 cup vinegar (I use rice vinegar)
1/8 teaspoon salt
1/4 ounce dried morels, brushed, reconstituted, and drained (liquid reserved)
3 tablespoons low-fat mayonnaise (homemade or prepared)
1 teaspoon freshly squeezed lemon juice
1/8–1/4 teaspoon Asian mustard
3/4 teaspoon fresh tarragon, finely chopped
1/4–1/2 teaspoon sea salt
1/2 teaspoon honey

Special Equipment:

Cookie press fitted with a swirl tip, or a pastry bag and tip
Food processor

Note: If using the yolk mixture as a "glue," you will need extra filling

Directions:

In a small nonstick sauté pan, add reconstituted morels and 2 tablespoons of reserved liquid; cook over medium heat for 8–9 minutes (adding more liquid if necessary during cooking process); stir frequently. When morels have absorbed all liquid, remove from heat and cool slightly; finely chop morels in a food processor or with a knife. Set aside.

In a 3-quart heavy pot or round Dutch oven, add quail eggs and cover with water; add vinegar and salt. Bring to boil over medium heat, 8–12 minutes depending on pan and amount of water. When it just begins to boil, set timer for 5 more minutes. Remove from heat and add cool water to the pan until the water is no longer hot (the eggs will still be warm).

Peel eggs while warm: taking one egg at a time, gently tap bottom of egg on edge of sink and gently push with fingers on all sides of the shell (the shell will be soft due to the vinegar); gently remove the shells under cool running water and place on paper toweling. Repeat process for remaining eggs. Place peeled and drained eggs in a container to chill completely.

When Ready to Stuff:

With a small sharp knife, cut hard-boiled quail eggs in half lengthwise, one at a time. Using both hands, gently push with your thumbs on the back of the half egg over a small bowl, while gently holding the edges of the egg white surrounding the yolk; the yolk will easily pop out.

Place all of the egg white halves on a tray, plate, or container whose sides are high enough to accommodate the eggs but shallow enough to fill them easily.

To the egg yolks, add the finely chopped morels, mayonnaise, lemon juice, Asian mustard, chopped tarragon, salt, and honey; mix all ingredients with the back of a fork until well combined. Place yolk mixture in a cookie press or pastry bag and carefully fill egg halves where the solid yolk was removed. *Note:* Don't overfill: make as decorative as desired, keeping the yolk mixture in the cavity.

Carefully cover with plastic wrap so wrap is not touching the filling; chill prior to serving.

Dim Sum Shrimp and Morel Dumplings

These little dumplings take time to make and need a while to steam, but they are worth every bit of the effort! Serve with Vinegar Dipping Sauce (see Additional Tips, p. 126) or your favorite Asian sauce. Perfect for an appetizer or for a light lunch entrée.

Yield: 34 filled dumplings or more, depending on how they are filled

Ingredients for the Filling:

1 1/4 ounces dried morels, brushed, reconstituted, and drained (liquid reserved)

1 pound fresh wild-caught shrimp (about 18), totally peeled and deveined

3 tablespoons finely chopped scallion, white and green parts

12 steamed pea pods (5 tablespoons), chopped

2 tablespoons fresh parsley, chopped

1 teaspoon sea salt

1 teaspoon chili oil

1 teaspoon olive oil

3/4 tablespoon grated fresh ginger

2 tablespoons Mirin (sweet Asian cooking wine)

Directions for Filling:

In a medium-sized nonstick sauté pan, add reconstituted morels and 1/4 cup of reserved liquid; cook over medium heat for 6–8 minutes (adding more liquid if necessary during cooking process); stir frequently. When morels have absorbed all liquid, remove from heat and cool slightly; when cool enough to handle, slice morels into rounds; set aside in a large glass bowl.

Coarsely chop raw shrimp into pieces (not minced) and place in the bowl with the morels; add chopped scallion and pea pods, along with the parsley, sea salt, chili oil, olive oil, ginger, and Mirin. Mix ingredients well and set aside; let marinate about 20 minutes.

Directions for Assembling Dumplings:

Have a small bowl of water handy for sealing your dumplings. Place one dumpling wrapper in the palm of your hand or on a flat surface. Put 1 heaping teaspoon of filling in the center of the circle; dip 2 fingers in the water and go around the outer edge of the circle. Fold in half, push down the filling to encase it with the wrappers, bring the edges together, and press the edges to seal the skin. Place thumbs in the center and bring the two side corners toward the center making a half-moon shaped "hat." Repeat with remaining wrappers and filling.

Coat the three bamboo steamers well with olive oil cooking spray and place each dumpling in one at a time with minimal space in between; repeat the process with the remaining dumplings. This should fill all three steamers.

In a wok or pot that will accommodate the steamer baskets, add cold water (several inches or more depending on the size of the pot). Place the stack of bamboo steamers with lid over boiling water and steam for 25 minutes or until the dumplings are transparent and the shrimp appears orange. Halfway through the cooking process, check the level of the water. If it looks low, lift the lid and pour boiling water over the top of the dumplings; replace the lid. Steaming time depends on pot used and level of water; it could take less time—just keep checking it!

When dumplings are transparent, remove the steamers and serve with an offering of sauce.

Ingredients for the Dumpling Wrappers:

Olive oil cooking spray

1 package (16-ounce) dumpling wrappers, Shanghai style (round)—3 1/2 inches in diameter

Special Equipment:

3 bamboo steamers (12 inches in diameter, 10 1/4-inch interior size).

Wok or pot to accommodate the steamers (leave clearance between the steamer and the water)

Flatbread Appetizers with Morel and Chive Schmear

This morel-infused Schmear (spread) is great as an appetizer on mini-bagels, toasted pita chips, bialies, toast, naan, lavash, or warm corn chips. Also, a great accompaniment to or ingredient in scrambled eggs. Make it spicy or keep it tame! Try making some homemade chèvre and use it here instead of the cream cheese. Fish allergies? You can always leave out the anchovies and add a pinch of salt!

Yield: about 1 cup

Ingredients:

3/4 ounce dried morels, brushed, reconstituted and drained (liquid reserved)

Olive oil cooking spray

3/4 cup light cream cheese or chèvre cheese

1/2 cup sliced fresh chives

3 tablespoons fresh chopped parsley leaves

2 teaspoons capers, drained

2–3 anchovies, drained

1/8 teaspoon cayenne

Tabasco® or red pepper sauce (optional)

Flatbread of your choice

Directions:

In a large nonstick sauté pan coated with cooking spray, cook morels over medium heat for about 9 minutes adding 1/4 cup of reserved morel liquid during the cooking process. The liquid will be absorbed at the end of cooking time. Set aside and cool.

In a food processor, process the cream cheese or chèvre, chives, parsley, capers, anchovies, and cayenne, just enough to chop and fully combine all ingredients. Add morels and pulse just to combine. For a spicier twist add a few drops Tabasco® or red pepper sauce. Spread on pieces of crisp flatbread, bagel chips, or bread or corn product of your choice.

The ingredients in these nontraditional tortilla-filled quesadillas are surprising and delicious. They can be served as an appetizer or a luncheon entrée. The combination of figs, morels, parsley, and brie is a melding of wonderful earthy ingredients—like eating chutney in a cheesy tortilla! No fresh figs? Pick up some dried and reconstitute with boiled water. Cook the quesadillas in a skillet or place in a tabletop panini machine until warm and crisp.

Crispy Fresh Fig, Morel, and Brie Quesadillas

Directions:

Preheat oven or toaster oven to 350°F. Set oven rack to middle position.

In a medium-sized nonstick sauté pan, add reconstituted morels and 1/4 cup of reserved liquid; cook over medium heat for 6–8 minutes (adding more liquid if necessary during cooking process), stirring frequently. When morels have absorbed all liquid, remove from heat and cool slightly. Finely chop morels in a food processor or with a knife and set aside.

In a small baking dish coated with olive oil cooking spray, place cleaned figs in one layer. Bake for about 30 minutes, or until soft (not mushy); set aside. When cool enough to handle, slice each in 3 or 4 slices; set aside.

Arrange tortillas on a flat surface. On half of each, add diced cheese, chopped morels, parsley, and fig slices, dividing equally. Fold over each tortilla.

In a large nonstick skillet coated with cooking spray, brown the quesadillas over medium-high heat on both sides until golden, or to desired doneness. As an alternative, use a panini machine. Cut each quesadilla into 2 or 3 wedges and transfer to small serving plates. Serve quesadillas warm and crisp, accompanied by fat-free heavy yogurt, if you like.

Yield: 8 quesadillas

Ingredients:

1 1/4 ounces dried morels, brushed, reconstituted, and drained (liquid reserved)

Olive oil cooking spray

15–16 small ripe mission figs (or figs of your choice), rinsed well and hard stem ends removed

8 (6-inch-diameter) flour tortillas (homemade or prepared), preferably fat-free

8 ounces brie, rind removed and cut into small dice

2 tablespoons freshly chopped parsley

Morel and Crab Tartlet Appetizers

This impressive appetizer or first course is perfect for formal or informal gatherings. One tartlet per guest is quite sufficient! Use your favorite cookie-cutter shapes for the tops of these delicious tartlets.

Yield: 6 tartlets

Ingredients:
Olive oil cooking spray
Pie pastry for a 9-inch crust (homemade or prepared), rolled out thin (between 1/8-inch–1/4-inch thickness)
2 tablespoons olive oil
8 ounces fresh morels, lightly brushed, rinsed, and drained
1/2 cup sliced scallion (white and green parts)
1 1/2 cups fresh, frozen, or preserved lump crabmeat (large chunks)
1/4 cup fat-free half-and-half
1 egg (slightly beaten)
1 teaspoon dried dill
1/4 teaspoon finely ground sea salt

Special Equipment:
6 small fluted tartlet pans (3 3/4 inches)
Circle cutter or top of a can or container that is a 4-inch round
Cookie sheet

Directions:
Preheat oven to 350°F. Set oven rack to middle position.

Coat each tartlet pan with cooking spray; set aside.

Cut out 6 circles, 4 inches in diameter, from the rolled out pastry dough. Place one circle of dough evenly in each tartlet pan, pressing around to make sure dough goes into the fluted sides and is even all around. With the tines of a fork, dock (pierce) the dough on the bottom 3 or 4 times; set aside. With the remaining dough, cut little shapes of any design for the top of the tartlet; set aside.

In a sauté pan, add 2 tablespoons of olive oil and heat to medium; add the whole morels and sauté for 8 minutes, stirring gently to sauté on all sides. Add the scallions and continue to cook for about 2 minutes. Set aside to cool.

Once cool, chop or process the morels and scallions to rough chop. In a medium-sized bowl, combine the chopped morels and scallions, crab, half-and-half, egg, dill, and salt. Mix with a fork until all of the ingredients are well combined.

Add about 1/3 cup of the crabmeat and morel mixture to each tartlet pan, dividing the filling evenly. Top each tartlet with a few cut-out dough shapes and place in the oven to bake for 60–70 minutes, or until the crust is lightly browned.

Let tartlets cool slightly and then gently turn out onto individual plates. Serve warm.

A twist on a favorite French salt cod dish, this version of brandade includes morels, potatoes, and smoked trout. Perfectly served with biscuits, crisp flatbread, or toasted baguette slices. Roast a whole bulb of garlic for this dish and use as much of it as desired—any left over, you can use it to spread on crusty pieces of bread with another meal.

Morel and Smoked-Trout Brandade

Directions:

In a large nonstick sauté pan over medium heat, cook morels with about 1/4 cup of reserved liquid for about 9 minutes, stirring occasionally until morels are cooked and liquid is absorbed. When cool to the touch, cut morels into round slices and set aside.

Coat garlic bulb with olive oil cooking spray. Bake garlic bulb in a 400°F oven for 30 minutes or until cloves are soft. Set aside. Peel or squeeze cloves when cool.

In a medium-sized saucepan filled with water, boil potatoes 30 minutes or until fork tender. Set aside.

Reduce oven to 350°F. Coat an ovenproof dish with cooking spray.

In the bowl of an electric mixer fitted with whisk attachment, add garlic cloves, cooked potatoes, half-and-half, flaked trout, and white pepper. When thoroughly mixed, add olive oil and stir. Add morels and stir, just to mix.

Place potato and morel mixture into the ovenproof dish and top with panko, if desired. Bake Morel and Smoked-Trout Brandade for 20–25 minutes or until mixture is warmed through. Serve with an array of biscuits and toast slices.

Yield: about 3 cups

Ingredients:

1 1/2 ounces dried morels, brushed, reconstituted and drained (liquid reserved)

4 cloves garlic, baked (see directions)

3 large baking potatoes (russet), peeled, rinsed, and quartered

1 1/4 cups fat-free half-and-half warmed (not boiled) with a bay leaf (after warming remove bay leaf)

2 smoked trout fillets (1 pound), skinned, boned, and flaked

1/4 teaspoon white pepper

2 tablespoons olive oil

Olive oil cooking spray

1/2 cup whole wheat panko (optional)

Morel- and Scallion-Filled Ebelskivers

A traditional Danish filled round (orblike) pancake transformed into a healthy appetizer, these are definitely work, but what a delicious savory result! Well worth the effort.

You do need a special pan for this dish—but a great one to have—An Ebelskiver (Abelskiver) pan. Both Nordic Ware nonstick pan and Lodge Cast Iron pans work great.

Yield: 42 filled savory pancake orbs

Ingredients for the Filling:
Olive oil cooking spray
2 ounces dried morels, brushed and reconstituted (liquid reserved)
3/4 cup chopped scallions (both dark and light green parts)
Mirin (sweet Asian cooking wine)
Sea salt

Directions for the Filling:
Drain morels. In a medium-sized sauté pan coated with cooking spray, sauté the morels for about five minutes. Add scallions and splash with a little Mirin. Sprinkle with a pinch of salt. Continue to cook just until scallions wilt. Remove from heat and set aside until ready to use as filling for the pancakes.

Directions for the Batter:
In a medium bowl, add both flours, baking powder, and salt; set aside.

In a small bowl, using a whisk, lightly beat the egg yolks, then whisk in the half-and-half, water, agave nectar, 2 tablespoons of melted butter, and olive oil. Whisk the yolk mixture into the dry ingredients until thoroughly combined.

Using a stand mixer with the whisk attachment, beat the egg whites on high until they become stiff but not dry (2–3 minutes). Using a rubber spatula, lightly stir the egg whites into the batter in several additions, At the end, whisk by hand to make sure everything is well combined.

Place 1/4 teaspoon of olive oil in each well of the Ebelskiver pan. Set over medium heat until the oil begins to bubble. Pour 1 tablespoon of batter into each well, about a third full. Place approximately a heaping teaspoon of filling in the center of each pancake. Top with an additional tablespoon of batter or use your pancake pen to fill to almost full. Cook until the bottoms are golden brown and crispy (3–5 minutes).

Using 2 wooden chopsticks or Ebelskiver tool, flip the pancakes over to brown the remaining side and cook about 3 minutes more. Transfer completed pancakes to a pan and repeat with remaining ingredients.

Serve immediately when all are made.

Ingredients for the Batter:
1 cup all-purpose flour
1 cup whole wheat flour
1 teaspoon baking powder
1/2 teaspoon sea salt
4 large eggs, separated
1 cup fat-free half-and-half
1 cup water
1 tablespoon agave nectar (or
    substitute sugar or other dry
    sweetener; if so add to the first
    set of pancake ingredients)
2 tablespoons unsalted butter,
    melted
2 tablespoons light olive oil
Light olive oil for oiling pan (1/4
    teaspoon per well)

Special Equipment:
Nonstick or cast-iron Ebelskiver pan
Pancake pen (optional), to pour
    batter neatly into the wells
Bamboo skewers, chopsticks, or
    a plastic shrimp deveiner for
    turning pancakes. (If using
    the cast-iron pan, use a small
    rounded table knife to release and
    turn the pancakes.)

Mushroom and Mussel Croquettes

A fabulous use of leftover mussels, or steam them just for this recipe. These croquettes are delicate, so proceed gently and they will come out fabulously! While they don't need a sauce, you can certainly add one—see below.

Yield: 24 croquettes

Ingredients:
8 ounces (about 52 mussels) cooked mussels without shells (previously steamed in white wine and spices), beards removed, and rough chopped
Olive oil cooking spray
1/2 cup shallots, peeled and finely chopped
1 ounce dried morels, brushed and reconstituted (liquid reserved)
2 eggs, beaten
1 teaspoon freshly squeezed lemon juice
1/2 teaspoon sea salt
1/4 teaspoon cayenne
1 1/2 cup whole wheat panko, divided
1/4 cup (or more, only if necessary) olive oil, for sautéing the croquettes

Sauce suggestion: Mix together
1/2 cup light mayonnaise (or 1/4 cup light mayonnaise and 1/4 cup fat-free sour cream)
1/2 cup sweetened Asian chili sauce
1 teaspoon grainy prepared mustard

Directions:

Place prepared mussels in a large nonreactive bowl.

In a medium-sized nonstick sauté pan coated with cooking spray, sauté the chopped shallots for about 3 minutes. Remove shallots to cool. To the same pan, add the reconstituted morels and sauté for about 6 minutes—adding 2–3 tablespoons of the reserved mushroom liquid. When cooked, remove from pan to cool. When cooled, rough chop by hand or pulse in a food processor.

In a large bowl with the mussels, add cooked morel mushrooms, sautéed shallots, lemon juice, sea salt, cayenne, beaten eggs, and 1/2 cup of the panko; stir thoroughly to combine. Allow croquette mixture to rest 15–20 minutes.

Place remaining cup of panko in a shallow dish. Form croquette mixture into large walnut-sized balls; roll them in the panko, covering all sides. This is a gentle process; they are delicate!

In a large nonstick sauté pan add olive oil over medium heat; when oil is hot, gently add the croquettes and cook 1 1/2–2 minutes on each side or until golden brown. Remove to a baking sheet lined with paper towels. Serve while warm with or without a sauce.

This delicious recipe is quick and easy, but oh so elegant! If you don't have enough mushrooms (which can happen), coat small Asian clay teacups with cooking spray and fill with enough crabmeat stuffing to appear full (about 1 1/2 tablespoons crab stuffing)—or use any other small dish that is ovenproof.

Crab- and Ramp-Stuffed Morels

Directions:
Preheat the oven to 350°F. Set oven rack to middle position.

In a medium-sized mixing bowl, flake crabmeat slightly. To the crabmeat, add half-and-half, mayonnaise, bread crumbs, sautéed ramps or shallots, egg yolk, sea salt, and cayenne. Using a fork, stir all crabmeat ingredients to mix well. Gently fill each morel with an adequate amount of crabmeat stuffing. You can use the tip of a rounded knife for this process to make sure stuffing goes to the top of the mushroom.

Coat a sauté pan with 2 tablespoons of olive oil; heat over medium heat. Place the stuffed morels in the sauté pan; gently and quickly, sauté the stuffed morels, turning on all sides to ensure they are evenly browned (but don't overcook). Place stuffed morels in an ovenproof dish or on small baking sheet. Bake the stuffed morels for 10 minutes, or until heated through.

Yield: depends on size of morels

Ingredients:
Olive oil cooking spray
1 1/2 cups lump crabmeat (large chunks of crab)
2 tablespoons fat-free half-and-half
1 1/2 tablespoons low-fat mayonnaise (homemade or prepared)
3 tablespoons finely processed bread crumbs (Italian-flavored or plain)
2 tablespoons sautéed chopped ramps (white part) or shallots until golden brown, and cooled
1 large egg yolk
1/4 teaspoon finely ground sea salt
1/8 teaspoon ground cayenne
Medium–large fresh morels, cleaned, gently rinsed, and stems removed (if openings are small, cut a little beyond the stem)
2 tablespoons olive oil

Note: If using clay teacups (or other ovenproof dishes) for extra stuffing, bake the filled cups for 20 minutes in total or until crabmeat stuffing is cooked through and just lightly browned on top.

Morel, Spinach, and Stilton Holiday Tart

Stilton cheese—an English favorite, made from cow's milk and blue veined with an undertone of Cheddar, crumbly in texture, and mellower than other blues—sits center stage with the morels in this unusual appetizer. You can substitute the Stilton with a domestic blue if desired (it will taste a bit stronger). This tart makes a perfect winter holiday appetizer! If making it in spring, use fresh morels. And, it can be enjoyed as part of any celebration or luncheon entrée.

Yield: 1 tart, 12–16 appetizer-sized servings

Ingredients:

1 ounce dried morels, brushed, reconstituted, and drained (liquid reserved)
Olive oil cooking spray
3 tablespoons peeled, finely chopped shallots
Pastry for 10-inch tart shell (homemade or prepared)
Egg wash—1 egg plus 1 tablespoon cold water
1/2 cup cooked and well-drained chopped spinach (squeeze all water out)
4 1/2 ounces Stilton (preferably Colston Basset), crumbled
3 eggs, slightly beaten
1 2/3 cups fat-free half-and-half
3/4 teaspoon finely ground sea salt
1/8 teaspoon finely ground cayenne

Directions:

Preheat the oven to 400°F. Set oven rack to middle position. Cover rack with aluminum foil in case of leakage.

In a medium-sized nonstick sauté pan coated with cooking spray, sauté the morels for about 6 minutes. Set aside; when cool, cut into halves lengthwise or keep whole if small.

Coat tart pan with olive oil cooking spray. Place rolled-out pastry dough evenly over a tart pan with removable bottom. Trim off any excess pastry dough from top of tart pan. *Note:* A rolling pin works well for trimming off excess dough (rolling it across the top).

Place a circle of parchment paper over dough (inside of tart) and weigh down with pie weights. Bake the tart shell for 15 minutes. When cool enough to handle, remove the parchment and weights. Brush the inside of the tart generously with the egg wash. Return to oven for 3–4 minutes to seal the lining. *Note:* If tart crust is not sealed, it will leak!

Lower oven temperature to 375°F.

Place the finely chopped shallots and morels evenly over the bottom of the tart; add spinach. Sprinkle crumbled Stilton over vegetables and morels.

In a glass bowl, thoroughly whisk together the eggs, half-and-half, sea salt, and cayenne. Pour cream mixture over vegetables, morels, and cheese.

Place tart in oven and bake 55–60 minutes or until puffy and lightly brown in color. Remove from oven and let set a few minutes before serving.

David Mcall
Johnston.

Special Equipment:
Tart pan with removable bottom
Parchment paper cut to fit the
    bottom inside of your tart
Pie weights (you can use raw rice or
    dry beans)
Aluminum foil
A large cake peel or lifter (such as
    used in pizza ovens) is great for
    transferring the tart from counter
    to oven (optional)

Crisp Panko, Morel, and Shrimp Appetizer

This crispy appetizer is for a special occasion—more olive oil is used in preparation than I normally use in this cookbook. Serve on small decorative appetizer plates with sprigs of fresh cilantro and dipping sauce.

Yield: 4 servings

Ingredients for Morels and Shrimp:
8 good-sized fresh morels, gently brushed and wiped clean (if small, increase number)
1 large egg plus 1 tablespoon water for egg wash, whisked and divided in half
1 1/4 cups panko (have extra on hand if necessary)
12 large (not jumbo) fresh shrimp, peeled, deveined, with tails left on for easy handling
1/4 cup olive oil
Sea salt
Cilantro for garnish

Ingredients for Dipping Sauce:
1/2 cup low-sugar or all-fruit apricot preserves
3 tablespoons seasoned rice vinegar
3/4 teaspoon Chinese mustard (or hot Chinese mustard powder), or to taste

Directions for the Morels and Shrimp:
Gently place morels in egg wash, then roll in panko; set finished morels on platter until ready to cook. Repeat the process with the shrimp (by holding by their tails).

In a medium-sized nonstick sauté pan, heat olive oil over medium until hot. Gently add the morels and cook until nicely browned on one side. Turn over and repeat process until the second side is also brown. Repeat the entire process with the shrimp. Drain on paper towels to remove any excess oil. Lightly salt if desired.

Directions for Dipping Sauce:
In a small bowl, combine preserves, vinegar, and mustard; whisk until smooth. Place three shrimp and two morels on each of four small appetizer plates. Serve with dipping sauce and sprigs of cilantro.

This is one of those special appetizers—a big statement! Savory and delicious, it will wow your guests. Slice carefully and keep the servings thin; this cheesecake is very rich.

Savory Morel Cheesecake

Directions:

Preheat oven to 325°F. Place oven rack to middle position.

Grease springform pan with butter substitute or cooking spray.

Coat the inside of the springform pan with the bread crumbs, tilting and tapping to cover evenly. Shake out any excess.

In a large nonstick sauté pan over medium heat, melt the butter substitute; add onion and sauté until transparent, 6–8 minutes. Add celery and cook until tender and onions are browned (4–5 minutes). Let cool slightly.

In the bowl of a food processor, process all of the cream cheese until smooth, about 2 minutes.

Add eggs, Jarlsberg cheese, half-and-half–water mixture, salt, and Tabasco®; process until ingredients are well blended.

Remove processor bowl and stir in the separately cooked morels and onion–celery mixture. Mix well. Pour the cheese and mushroom mixture into the prepared springform pan.

Set springform pan in a large roasting pan or ovenproof container; fill pan with enough cool water (bain marie) to come halfway up the sides of the springform pan (do not overfill). Bake for 1 hour and 20–25 minutes. Turn the oven off and leave the cheesecake in the oven with the door slightly ajar for an additional hour (this prevents cracking).

Remove springform pan from the roaster and place on a wire rack to cool fully.

Once cooled, remove sides of the springform pan and serve at room temperature.

If not serving immediately, keep cheesecake in the refrigerator covered with plastic wrap. Bring back to room temperature before serving. Return any remaining cheesecake to the refrigerator for storage, keeping it well covered.

Yield: 1 savory cheesecake, 12–16 servings

Ingredients:

3 tablespoons butter substitute, plus more for greasing pan (*Note:* you can use olive oil cooking spray for pan instead of additional butter substitute)

Finely ground bread crumbs, homemade or prepared

1 1/2 cups finely chopped sweet yellow onion

1/4 cup finely chopped celery

3 packages (24 ounces) light cream cheese

4 large eggs

1 cup freshly grated Jarlsberg cheese

1/4 cup fat-free half-and-half, plus one tablespoon water

1/2 teaspoon sea salt (or more to taste)

2 teaspoons Tabasco® or red pepper sauce (or more to taste)

2 cups fresh morels, sautéed for 8–9 minutes in butter substitute and sliced into rounds

Special Equipment:

9-inch springform pan (with tight seal)

Note: Reconstitute dried morels if fresh are not available. Proceed as directed in recipe; just be sure to cook mushrooms after reconstituting.

Shrimp, Morel, and Edamame Chilled Salad

This fresh and gingery light salad is great as an appetizer, side dish, or lunch entrée. If feeling exotic, serve in a ripe half avocado or a half of a cantaloupe or honeydew melon.

Yield: 6 servings

Ingredients for the Dressing:
1 clove fresh garlic, peeled and minced
1 1/2 tablespoons freshly grated ginger (or purchased Gourmet Garden Ginger Spice Blend)
5 tablespoons seasoned rice vinegar
1/4 teaspoon sea salt
3 tablespoons olive oil

Ingredients for the Salad:
1 1/2 cups cooked morels (fresh or reconstituted), cooked, chilled, and cut into rounds
1 cup of shelled cooked edamame
2 cups of cooked and chilled fresh shrimp, cut into small bite-sized pieces
1 cup thinly sliced celery
1/4 cup thinly sliced scallion or chives
Sesame seeds for garnish (tricolor sesame seeds if possible—white, black, and wasabi)
Large lettuce leaves or fresh spinach

Directions for the Dressing:
In a bowl or small food processor, combine garlic, ginger, rice vinegar, and salt. Process until well mixed. Slowly add in olive oil in a steady stream until all ingredients are combined.

Directions for the Salad:
In a large nonreactive bowl, toss the cooked morels, edamame, shrimp pieces, celery, and scallion or chives. Add dressing and toss thoroughly. Serve on a large lettuce leaf or a bed of fresh spinach.

Smoked Salmon, Morel, and Scallion Pâté

This flavorful appetizer spread is fabulous on toast points, biscuits, baguette, or fresh vegetables. You can also use it as a filling for pasta or fresh morels!

Directions:

In a large sauté pan coated with cooking spray, cook morels over medium heat for about 9 minutes, adding 1/4 cup of reserved morel liquid during the cooking process. The morel liquid will be absorbed at the end of cooking time. Allow to cool.

In a food processor, process the cooked morels, smoked salmon, chèvre cheese, scallions, and the 2 tablespoons of additional morel liquid—just enough to fully combine and chop all ingredients.

Place finished appetizer spread in a bowl to serve. Garnish with chopped chives or additional scallions if desired.

Ingredients:

1 ounce dried morels, brushed, reconstituted, and drained (liquid reserved)

Olive oil cooking spray

1/4 cup plus 2 tablespoons reserved morel liquid, divided

6 ounces wild smoked salmon (preferably sockeye)

1 log chèvre cheese (11 ounces), cut into chunks

1/2 cup scallions (white and green parts), cut into slices

1 tablespoon chopped chives (for garnish if desired)

Note: Make great toast shapes by rolling out slices of bread with a rolling pin and cutting desired shapes with cookie cutters. Bake shapes on a baking sheet until crisp and serve with the pâté

Wild Mushroom Crostini

These crostini are crisp and flavorful—great for a party appetizer (plan on 4–5 per guest) or just as a snack. Feel free to use the wild mushrooms of your choice with your morels. Wild Mushroom Crostini can easily be served alone or with an accompaniment of other appetizers–they are great with an array of cheese, seasonal fruit, or hard-boiled quail eggs.

For a special treat, top each mushroom crostini with a shard of Parmigiano–Reggiano before putting it under the broiler.

Yield: At least 30 rounds, depending on the size of your baguette and slices.

Ingredients:
2 ounces dried wild mushrooms of your choice, brushed, reconstituted, and drained (liquid reserved)
1 baguette, sliced in rounds (about 1/2-inch thick)
1 leek (white and light green part only), rinsed, sliced in thin rounds, rinsed again, and drained
1 1/2 tablespoons olive oil
2 tablespoons Triple Sec
1/4 teaspoon sea salt (or to taste)
2 tablespoons (or more) RMJ's Garlic Essence (see Additional Tips, p. 126)

Special Equipment:
Pastry or silicone brush

Directions:
Preheat the broiler. Set oven rack to top section of the oven.

In a medium-sized nonstick sauté pan over medium-high heat, add olive oil and leeks; sauté for 3 minutes or until lightly brown. Remove leeks from pan and set aside.

In the same pan over medium-high heat, sauté the reconstituted mushrooms with 1/2 cup of reserved liquid for about 6 minutes (making sure all mushrooms are soft); add Triple Sec and continue to cook for an additional 2–3 minutes.

Let mushrooms cool slightly; place the mushrooms and leeks in the bowl of a food processor; process on pulse to chop; set aside.

Place the baguette bread slices on a baking tray and place under the broiler for a couple of minutes just to crisp the top of the bread slices; remove from oven. Turn all of the bread slices over and brush each untoasted side with some Garlic Essence; replace under the broiler for just a minute or two until bubbly (don't brown).

Top each slice of baguette with the wild mushroom and leek mixture; press down gently, making sure to cover the whole surface of the baguette. Place all covered baguette slices back under the broiler and heat for a few minutes just to warm.

Serve immediately.

Soft-shell crabs are a favorite spring and summertime treat. These can also be served as an entrée on a small bed of greens or wild rice with a nice wedge of lemon. Serve one to a guest, two, or three . . . they are so good and crunchy that guests will beg for more!

Morel and Parmigiano–Reggiano-Dusted Soft-Shell Crab

Directions:

To clean the crabs: With sturdy kitchen shears, cut across face of the crab, behind the eyes and mouth. Lift the pointed sides of the crab and remove the gills on both sides (one side at a time). Turn crab over, and on the bottom side, remove tail flap (apron). Rinse each crab thoroughly with cool water. Pat crabs dry with paper toweling and set aside.

In a small bowl, combine the dried morel "dust," grated cheese, and flour. Add that mixture to a breading tray or other low-sided container. In a second breading tray, add the egg mixture.

Dip a prepared crab into egg mixture and then into the morel, cheese, and flour mixture; making sure crab is fully coated. Set completed crab on a plate; repeat the process with the remaining crabs.

Heat a large nonstick sauté pan with oil over medium-high heat. When hot, add crabs; cook for about 3 minutes until nicely golden, gently turn over, and cook the other side an additional 3 minutes. Remove from heat, set on paper toweling for a moment, and serve.

Yield: 6 soft-shell crabs

Ingredients:

6 fresh medium-sized soft-shell crabs
1/2 ounce dried morels, finely ground ("dust")
1/4 cup freshly grated Parmigiano–Reggiano cheese
1/2 cup whole wheat flour
1 whole egg, beaten with 1 tablespoon low-fat milk
1/4 cup tea seed oil (if possible, or any monounsaturated oil that is used for cooking at high temperatures)

Special Equipment:

Sturdy kitchen shears

David McCall Johnston

This special recipe makes one of those special occasion soups—rich and hearty. Serve with a huge chunk of crusty bread or place in individual bread bowls for a great presentation. Use ale that is not overpowering—while you want the flavor, you don't want it to overwhelm the dish or the morels.

Across-the-Pond—Inspired Potato and Morel Cheese Soup

Directions:

In a large nonstick sauté pan, heat 1 tablespoon olive oil over medium heat, add reconstituted morels and cook for about 8 minutes, stirring frequently. When cooked, set aside to cool slightly.

When cool enough to handle, slice morels into rounds and set aside.

In a large heavy stockpot or Dutch oven, heat remaining tablespoon of olive oil over medium heat and sauté onions. Cook onions for 10 minutes or until nicely browned. Add potatoes and cook for about 8 minutes. Add beef stock, morel liquid, and dark ale. Reduce heat to simmer and continue to cook for about 45 minutes. Add the cayenne and adjust seasonings. Turn off heat and add cheese. Process the soup with an immersion blender, Vita Mix®, or food processor until smooth.

Once soup is smooth, stir in morel rounds and reheat if necessary. Garnish with fresh chopped chives, if desired.

Yield: Big batch, 12–16 servings

Ingredients:

2 1/2 ounces dried morels, brushed, reconstituted, and drained (liquid reserved—at least 2 cups)
2 tablespoons olive oil, divided
4 large sweet yelllow onions, peeled and chopped
4 cups potatoes previously peeled and cubed
8 cups low-sodium beef stock (homemade or prepared)
2 cups reserved morel liquid
2 cups dark ale (preferable British)
2 cups low-fat (not fat-free) cheddar cheese
1/2 teaspoon cayenne
Chopped chives (for garnish, if desired)
Salt (optional—depending on saltiness of beef stock, and remember the cheese has salt)

Chicken Soup with Lemon, Morel, and Thyme Matzo Balls

Morel mushrooms, lemon, and thyme marry well with an old favorite—chicken soup. This twist on traditional Jewish fare offers a Passover staple or delicious soup any time of the year. Sorry traditional matzo ball devotees—no chicken fat here! These matzo balls are light and serve as a canvas for the prized morel. If you prefer a very dense matzo ball, reduce the amount of egg by half. Use homemade or prepared chicken stock (see Additional Tips for Chicken Stock recipe, p. 130).

Yield: 16 matzo balls

Ingredients:

1 ounce dried morels, brushed, reconstituted, and drained (liquid reserved)

4 large eggs

1/2 cup plain sparkling water or seltzer

3 tablespoons freshly squeezed lemon juice (Meyer lemons if possible)

4 tablespoons olive oil

1 teaspoon fresh lemon thyme leaves (or use regular fresh thyme and 1/2 teaspoon lemon juice), minced

1 1/4–1 1/2 teaspoons kosher salt

1/8–1/4 teaspoon white pepper

1 cup matzo meal

chicken stock (homemade or prepared)

Directions:

In a medium-sized nonstick sauté pan, add reconstituted morels and 1/4 cup of reserved liquid; cook over medium heat for about 8 minutes (adding more liquid if necessary during cooking process); stir frequently. When morels have absorbed all liquid, remove from heat and cool slightly; process in a food processor on pulse or chop with a knife. Set aside.

In a large nonreactive bowl, beat the eggs lightly with a whisk. Stir in the seltzer, lemon juice, olive oil, thyme, salt, and pepper. Gradually add the matzo meal, stirring until the mixture is well mixed. Cover the bowl with plastic wrap and refrigerate for a minimum of 2 hours. Remove from fridge and add the chopped morels; mix well.

Place a large round Dutch oven or stockpot nearly full of water over medium-high heat; bring to a boil. With wet hands, place approximately two tablespoons (or use a scoop that holds 2 tablespoons) of matzo ball mixture in the palms of your hands, Pat into a ball and drop into the boiling water. Repeat the process until all of the matzo–morel mixture is used. *Note:* Don't get them too wet from your hands.

When all the matzo balls are placed in the water, cover the pot and reduce the heat to medium-low (if the heat appears too hot after a few minutes, reduce it to low). Cook the matzo balls, covered, for 30 minutes—no peeking! Keeping the pot covered throughout the cooking process will prevent the matzo balls from falling apart.

After 30 minutes, gently remove the matzo balls from the pot and place one or two, in each soup bowl (depending on the size of the bowl), then add your chicken soup. If not using immediately, remove the matzo balls from the water and place on one layer on paper toweling; let cool slightly. Place them in a low-sided container (keeping them in one layer if possible); refrigerate until ready for use. Do not store them in the soup or they will become too soggy.

Speckled with parsley and carrot, colorful and earthy, this soup makes for a great first course or a luncheon entrée. Feel free to add more or less curry—just don't let it overpower this morel-infused soup. Add a dollop of heavy yogurt on top as a garnish or sprinkle with chopped nuts for a flavor and texture change.

Curried Cauliflower and Morel Soup

Directions:

In a large nonstick sauté pan coated with cooking spray, cook the morels over medium heat with about 1/2 cup of reserved liquid. Stir occasionally and continue to cook for 9 minutes or until liquid is absorbed. Remove from heat and set aside.

In a large stockpot or Dutch oven, heat oil over medium-high heat and sauté onions for 9 minutes or until lightly browned. Reduce heat to medium and add cauliflower. Continue to stir frequently for about 6 minutes. Add diced potato and cook another 6 minutes. Add vegetable stock and bring to a boil, about 20 minutes.

Reduce heat to simmer and cook an additional 20 minutes, until all vegetables are fork tender.

Turn off heat and process soup with an immersion blender, Vita Mix®, or food processor. Process the soup ingredients until smooth. *Note:* Depending on size of cauliflower, if soup appears too thick, stir in some additional vegetable stock to desired consistency.

Add curry and mix thoroughly. Stir into the soup the reserved cooked morels, parsley, and carrot. Adjust seasonings if necessary.

Heat gently until warmed through and flavors have had a chance to meld.

Serve in individual bowls and add a dollop (about 1 tablespoon) of heavy yogurt if desired.

Yield: 8–10 servings (depending on serving size)

Ingredients:

Olive oil cooking spray

2 ounces (or more) dried morels, brushed, reconstituted, and drained (liquid reserved)

1 1/2 tablespoons olive oil

1 large sweet yellow onion (about 2 cups), peeled and chopped

1 large fresh cauliflower, leaves and stem removed and rough chopped

3 small red potatoes, scrubbed clean (skins left intact) and diced (about 1 1/4 cups)

8 cups low-sodium vegetable stock (homemade or prepared)

2 teaspoons curry powder

4 tablespoons chopped flat-leaf parsley (no stems)

2 cups peeled, shredded raw carrot

Sea salt (depending on saltiness of stock)

Heavy yogurt (Laban, optional; see Additional Tips, p. 125)

Big-Batch Garden Vegetable and Wild Mushroom Soup

A great soup to make in the summer when vegetables are plentiful! Then you can freeze it in freezer-safe jars for winter. Feel free to mix and match vegetables that you have available in your own garden, or vegetables you prefer. Chanterelles are available fresh in the summer—use fresh if possible or use a combination of dried morels and chanterelles. You can certainly serve this soup year round, as a first course or luncheon entrée. Or add some protein and call it dinner!

Yield: 10–12 servings

Ingredients:

3 ounces dried morels, brushed, reconstituted, and drained (3 1/2–4 cups liquid reserved)

1 pound fresh chanterelle mushrooms, brushed or wiped clean, lightly rinsed, and drained

3 tablespoons olive oil, divided

1–2 large sweet yellow onions, peeled and cut into 1-inch pieces

4 cloves, garlic, peeled and finely minced

1–2 long finger pepper, seeded, deveined, and finely chopped

6–8 carrots, trimmed, peeled, and cut into bite-sized pieces

8–10 ribs celery, trimmed and cut into bite-sized pieces (leaves included)

24 okra (about 3 cups), trimmed and cut into bite-sized pieces

2 cans (28 ounces each) petite-diced tomatoes with juice, or fresh tomatoes (preferably Roma, diced and juice retained)

Directions:

In a large nonstick sauté pan over medium heat, cook reconstituted morels in 1/2 cup morel liquid for 8–9 minutes; set aside. When cool enough to handle, cut morels in half lengthwise. Put morels in a bowl and set aside. In the same pan, sauté the chanterelles in 1 tablespoon of olive oil over medium heat for about 8 minutes; set aside. When cool enough to handle, slice the chanterelles and place in the same bowl with the cooked morels; set aside.

In an extra large round Dutch oven or stockpot, add remaining 2 tablespoons of olive oil and heat to medium-high; add onions and cook until browned, about 6 minutes. Reduce heat to medium; add garlic and sauté for 1 minute. Add carrots and cook for 5 minutes, stirring frequently; add celery and cook 5 minutes. Add okra and cook 4 minutes; add pepper and stir for 1–2 minutes. *Note:* You are adding the hardest vegetables first.

Add tomatoes and stir about 2 minutes, mixing all ingredients.

Add beef or vegetable stock and bring to a boil (about 25 minutes); skim if necessary. Reduce heat to simmer and let cook for 2 hours, stirring occasionally. Add corn, all wild mushrooms, and fresh spices. Continue to cook for an additional hour (or longer), giving all flavors the opportunity to meld into a rich and flavorful soup. If it looks like there is not enough liquid, add more stock. Adjust seasonings as necessary and serve hot. *Note:* For winter meals, you may want to add your favorite hearty lean protein—beef, bison, venison, beans, or tofu). Make sure to have some crusty whole wheat bread to serve with your soup.

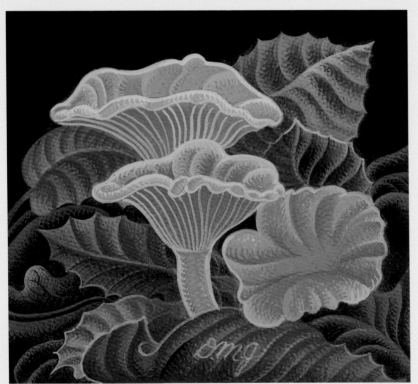

Courtesy Earthy Delights

6 cups beef stock or vegetable stock (homemade or prepared)

3 cups reserved morel liquid

1 large zucchini (about 3 cups), washed, trimmed, and shredded

4 ears corn, husk/silk removed, and kernels cut from the cob (about 2 cups of kernels)

1 tablespoon fresh chopped basil

1 tablespoon fresh chopped oregano

1 tablespoon fresh chopped lemon verbena (or lemon zest if no verbena is available)

1 tablespoon fresh chopped flat-leaf parsley

1/2–2 teaspoons kosher salt (depending on saltiness of stock)

Special Equipment:

Extra-large Dutch oven or stockpot (10–13 quarts)

Morel and Rosemary White Bean Soup

This delicious soup is substantial enough to serve as an entrée! Just add a crisp green salad and a slice of crusty whole wheat bread.

Morels with their woodsy flavor pair well with the rosemary and the flavored pork, which are both really used in this recipe as a seasoning. As morels also pair well with cream, this soup gives you the feeling of something creamy with no added milk product.

Yield: 12 servings

Ingredients for Soup:

1 lb. dry white beans (navy/ cannelini), sorted, rinsed, and soaked overnight (about 6 cups of cooked beans or three 15-ounce cans)

1 lb. pork loin, fat trimmed, rinsed, and patted dry

3 tablespoons hoisin sauce, homemade (see Additional Tips, p. 125) or prepared olive oil cooking spray

2 ounces dried morels, brushed, reconstituted, and drained (liquid reserved)

8–10 cups low-fat chicken stock (homemade or prepared)

2 tablespoons olive oil

2 large red onions, peeled and thinly sliced

3 cloves garlic, peeled and sliced

2 cups baby spinach

2–3 small sprigs fresh rosemary

Salt, if necessary (depending on saltiness of stock)

Directions:

As indicated in ingredient list, white beans need to be soaked overnight—make sure to refrigerate while they are soaking. Do not leave overnight on the counter!

Preheat oven to 350°F. Set oven rack to middle position.

Coat a small open roasting pan with cooking spray. Baste the pork loin with hoisin sauce and bake for 45 minutes or until the pork is at 165°F; set aside until cool enough to handle and then cut into small dice.

Coat a nonstick sauté pan with cooking spray. Once morels are reconstituted, drain and sauté for about 4 minutes over medium heat. Splash the morels with about 1/4 cup of chicken stock and continue to cook for an addition 5 minutes, or until all liquid is absorbed. When morels are cooked, set aside.

In a large stockpot or Dutch oven, heat 2 tablespoons of olive oil over medium heat and add onion; cook 9 minutes (stirring frequently) or until the onions begin to brown lightly.

Add garlic and continue to cook an additional minute.

Add reserved drained beans and sauté for about 2 minutes over medium heat.

Add 8 cups of chicken stock and let cook over medium heat until soup comes to a boil. Reduce heat to medium-low and continue to cook for an hour, or until the beans are tender.

With an immersion blender, Vita Mix®, or food processor, process the soup until smooth. Add baby spinach and reprocess just until soup is spotted with the green spinach.

Add cooked pork and let soup simmer about 15 minutes to incorporate flavors. Add the sprigs of rosemary and cooked morels; simmer again about 15 minutes. If soup appears too thick for your taste, stir in some reserved chicken stock to desired consistency.

Serve the soup in individual bowls or from a tureen.

Special Equipment:
Immersion blender, Vita Mix®, or
food processor

Note: This recipe requires overnight soaking of beans!

Purée of Asparagus Soup with Morels

This is a fresh and flavorful soup that is perfect for spring and summer months. Make sure your soup has enough body to hold the morel rounds—you want the texture a bit substantial, not too watery! Perfect for a light lunch or first course. Morel amount can be adjusted according to size of bowl

Yield: 8–10 (depending on serving size)

Ingredients for the Soup:
1 1/2 tablespoons olive oil
2 sweet yellow onions, peeled and sliced
2 1/4 pounds fresh asparagus, removing bottom 1 1/2 inches, rinsed, and cut into 1-inch pieces
8 cups low-sodium chicken stock (homemade or prepared)
3 large fresh mint leaves
1 teaspoon salt (optional depending on saltiness of stock)

Ingredients for the Morel Topping:
1 1/2 tablespoons low-calorie butter substitute or olive oil
8 medium-sized fresh morels per person (should equal 1/2 cup sliced morels per serving), brushed, lightly rinsed and drained

Special Equipment:
Immersion blender, Vita Mix®, or food processor

Directions:

In a large stockpot or Dutch oven, heat oil over medium-high and sauté onions 12–14 minutes or until lightly browned, reduce heat to medium, and add asparagus pieces. Cook for about 2 minutes, stirring frequently. Add chicken stock and let soup come to a boil (12 –15 minutes). Reduce heat to low and continue to simmer for 30 minutes. At about 45 minutes, add mint leaves and process soup with an immersion blender, Vita Mix®, or food processor. Process the soup ingredients until smooth. Adjust seasoning, if necessary.

In a large sauté pan over medium heat; add butter substitute or olive oil. When hot, add morels and cook for 6–8 minutes. When cool enough to handle, slice morels into rounds.

Reheat soup if necessary. Place hot soup in individual serving bowls, top each bowl with 1/2 cup of morel-slice topping, and serve.

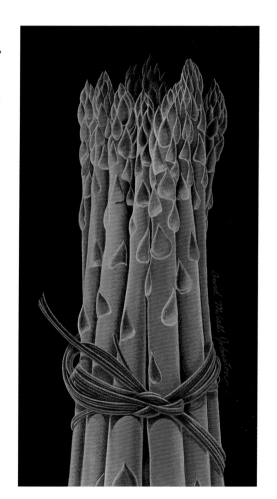

This big batch of delicious and elegant morel soup is a perfect appetizer for a large crowd. No milk or cream included in the recipe, but it is very creamy, and leftovers freeze well. Your guests will not realize there are white mushrooms in the recipe and will think this soup is made of "gold" with all the morels . . . keep the secret!

Big-Batch Morel Mushroom Soup

Directions:

With a sharp knife or kitchen shears, slice all the drained morels into rounds and place in a small bowl (reserving stems and other parts that are not perfect rounds).

Heat olive oil in a large heavy stockpot or Dutch oven over medium heat; add leeks and sauté until tender, 6–8 minutes. Add the reconstituted morel stems and imperfect bits and cook for 6–8 minutes, stirring frequently.

Add the sliced white mushrooms and continue to cook an additional 6 minutes.

Add the chicken stock and reserved morel water; bring all ingredients to a boil. Upon rapid boil, reduce heat and cover pot with a lid. Cook on medium-low and simmer for an additional 30 minutes.

In a large nonstick sauté pan, add the butter substitute and sauté the morels rounds until tender, 8–9 minutes. Set aside.

Remove the soup from the heat source and puree in batches with an immersion blender, Vita Mix®, or food processor, until very smooth; place back in the original pot. Add salt and pepper if necessary; mix and adjust seasonings. Reheat soup (if needed).

Top each bowl of soup with some of the sautéed morel rounds and scallion garnish. Serve.

Yield: 20–30 servings

Ingredients:

8 ounces dried morels, brushed, reconstituted, and drained (liquid reserved) *Note:* make sure to utilize at least 4 cups of boiling water in the reconstituting process

3 tablespoons olive oil

12 cups leeks, white part only, washed well and thinly sliced

10 cups white mushrooms, brushed, washed, and thinly sliced

20 cups low-sodium chicken stock (homemade or prepared)

4 cups reserved morel mushroom liquid, strained

3 tablespoons butter substitute

Salt to taste (depending on saltiness of stock)

1/8 teaspoon cayenne (optional)

Scallions, washed and sliced into thin rounds, for garnish

Special Equipment:

Immersion blender, Vita Mix®, or food processor

Clam and Morel Chowder

This creamy and hearty chowder will certainly double as an entrée with a crisp green salad and some crusty whole wheat rolls or some homemade oyster crackers! If you are short on morels, or want a little different twist of flavor, add a variety of wild mushrooms and prepare as directed.

Yield: 12 servings

Ingredients:

3 tablespoons olive oil (or low-fat butter substitute), divided
1 large, sweet yellow onion, peeled, and sliced or chopped
4 1/2 cups russet potatoes, peeled and cubed
10 cups clam or crab stock (Homemade or prepared—Minor's has great clam and crab soup bases)
2 cups celery ribs, chopped with leaves
6 cans (6.5 ounces each) chopped clams (no MSG), drained and clams rinsed
1 can (14 ounces) light coconut milk
3 ounces dried morels, brushed, reconstituted, and drained (liquid reserved)
Sea salt (if necessary depending on saltiness of stock)

Special Equipment:

Immersion blender, Vita Mix®, or food processor

Directions:

In a large nonstick sauté pan, heat 1 1/2 tablespoons olive oil over medium-high heat; add reconstituted morels and sauté for 6–8 minutes; set aside.

In a large stockpot or Dutch oven, heat remaining olive oil over medium heat and add onion; sauté for 8 minutes or until lightly brown. Add potatoes; sauté for a few minutes and add clam or crab stock. Continue to cook over medium heat for 30 minutes or until potatoes are fork tender.

With an immersion blender, Vita Mix®, or food processor, process the soup ingredients until smooth.

To the stock, add celery and cook for about 20 minutes. Add clams, coconut milk, and cooked morels. Continue to cook for 20 more minutes, until all ingredients and flavors meld. Check seasonings and adjust if necessary. Serve warm with rolls or oyster crackers.

The Shore

Thai Morel Bisque

An elegant appetizer with that woodsy morel Thai flavor! Great anytime of the year—for all soup fans. Serve as a first course, or use it as a centerpiece for a luncheon meal. (A few prawn crackers would make a great accompaniment to this flavorful soup.)

Yield: 6 servings

Ingredients:

2–3 tablespoons olive oil (or butter substitute)

2 bunches of scallions, white part only, finely sliced (reserve the green for garnish)

2 ounces dried morels, brushed, reconstituted, and drained (at least 1 cup liquid reserved)

4 cups low-sodium chicken stock (homemade or prepared)

1 cup strained reserved mushroom liquid

2 cups light coconut milk

1–2 Thai red peppers, washed and split

1/4 cup Mirin (sweet Asian cooking wine)

Salt to taste

Fresh chopped cilantro and chopped scallion for garnish

Directions:

Heat 1 tablespoon of olive oil (or butter substitute) in a medium-sized nonstick sauté pan. Add morels and sauté for about 4 minutes, stirring and turning the mushrooms to cook evenly. Remove from pan and set aside until slightly cool. Slice morels into rounds. Set aside.

To the same nonstick sauté pan, add the white parts of the scallions and sauté for about 2 minutes, then remove and add to morel rounds.

In a separate medium-large pot, heat the remaining olive oil (or butter substitute), add 2 tablespoons of flour and sauté until it becomes bubbly and slightly brown. Slowly add chicken stock, coconut milk, red pepper(s), and Mirin; continue to stir. Let stock mixture simmer gently for about 15 minutes. Add morels and scallions.

Let the flavors of the bisque meld on low for about 20 minutes. In the last two minutes, add cilantro and chopped green scallion.

Ladle Thai Morel Bisque into bowls and serve.

This twist on a traditional Thai-flavored soup makes a great first course or a full entrée for 6 guests. Flavorful and light, the morels make a great statement! Feel free to add or subtract any Asian vegetables; use what you have or purchase your favorites. And make sure to find the lowest-sodium fish sauce possible!

Morel, Chicken, and Shrimp Tom Kha Kai Soup

Directions:

In a large stock pot over medium heat, bring to a boil 8 cups low-sodium chicken stock, Thai fish sauce, lemongrass, Thai basil or kaffir lime leaves, and galangal, about 12 minutes. Stir well, reduce heat, and simmer 20–25 minutes.

While the stock is simmering, prepare the morels. In a medium-large nonstick sauté pan coated with olive oil, cook morels for about 6 minutes, adding a little morel liquid during the cooking process. When cooked, set morels aside. Return to the soup stock and strain if desired (in Thailand it is not strained, although the lemongrass, lime leaves, and galangal are not meant to be eaten).

Add to the simmered stock the white part of the scallions, pea pods, cooked morels, spinach or napa, bok choy, chicken breast meat, coconut milk, and small red peppers; return to boil, 6–7 minutes. Add shrimp to the mixture and continue to simmer until the chicken and shrimp are cooked through, about 2 more minutes. Do not over cook meats! Add lime juice and serve garnished with scallion greens and fresh cilantro leaves.

Yield: 12 servings

Ingredients:

8 cups low-fat/low-sodium chicken stock (homemade or prepared)
1/3 cup plus 1 tablespoon fish sauce
3 thick sections of whole lemongrass, peeled, trimmed, and cut into 3-inch pieces
4 Thai basil or kaffir lime leaves (optional)
2-inch section of galangal, peeled
Olive oil
1 1/2 ounces dried morels, brushed, reconstituted, and halved (liquid reserved)
1/2 cup white part of scallions (use green part for garnish)
20 pea pods, cut into bite-sized pieces
4 cups baby spinach or chopped napa cabbage
3 cups sliced Thai bok choy
3/4 pound raw chicken breast, sliced
3/4 pound raw shrimp, peeled and deveined
2 (14 ounce) cans light coconut milk
3–6 small red Thai chilies, slightly crushed or slit open
Juice of 2 limes or of 1 Meyer lemon

Morel Spill

ENTRÉES

This halibut has a pocket that is stuffed with morels, leeks, and carrots. Have your local fishmonger cut the pocket (a slice cut about halfway through) if you are concerned about doing it yourself or don't have a really sharp kitchen knife.

Baked Halibut with a Pocket of Morels, Scallions, and Carrots

Directions:

Preheat oven to 350°F. Set oven rack to middle position.

In a medium-sized nonstick sauté pan coated with cooking spray, heat over medium-high heat; add morels and about 1/4 cup reserved morel liquid. Cook about 6 minutes; remove from heat. When cool enough to handle, cut into slices lengthwise; set aside.

On a clean flat surface, lay halibut with pocket open. Place shards of carrot on flesh of fish; top with a layer of leek slices and then most of the cooked morel rounds (reserve some for the top). Fold flap down so halibut appears stuffed with the vegetables and morels. Coat with cooking spray a low, relatively small baking dish that will comfortably accommodate the fish; place stuffed fish in center of the dish, and drizzle with olive oil. Pour Mirin and lemon juice over the fish; sprinkle with tarragon.

Bake for about 40 minutes, depending on thickness of fish. Halfway through the baking process, add the reserved morel slices to top of fish and sprinkle with sea salt; continue baking. Remove from baking pan and place on a platter for serving.

Yield: 4 servings

Ingredients:

Olive oil cooking spray

3/4 ounces morels, brushed, reconstituted, and drained (liquid reserved)

1 pound halibut, with a pocket cut halfway through, lightly rinsed with cool water and patted dry

3/4 cup shards of carrot (cut with a peeler), about 2 1/2 inches in length

3 leeks (white and light green part only), about 2 1/2 inches each, halved and cut again into thin strips

1 1/2 tablespoons olive oil

1/4 cup Mirin (sweet Asian cooking wine)

1/8 cup freshly squeezed lemon juice (preferably Meyer lemon)

2 teaspoons chopped fresh tarragon

1/4 teaspoon sea salt

Baked Rosemary Herbed Chicken with Cider–Morel Sauce

This delicious baked chicken has a real rosemary essence. Serve with a small amount of the Cider–Morel Sauce—very rich!! Perfect for company or a special dinner at home. This delicious sauce is also great on pork, duck, goose, and rabbit.

Yield: Serves 4–6 (depending on size of chicken)

Ingredients for the Baked Chicken:
Olive oil cooking spray
4–5 pound chicken, bag containing neck and giblets removed, rinsed in cool water and patted dry
1 large sweet yellow onion, peeled, rinsed, and quartered
Olive oil
Fresh rosemary sprigs (2–3 inch pieces)
2 teaspoons Chinese five-spice powder (or more to taste)

Ingredients for the Cider–Morel Sauce:
4 cups apple cider
1 1/2 ounces dried morels, brushed, reconstituted (liquid reserved), and morels cut in half lengthwise
1 tablespoon olive oil
1/4 cup minced shallots
1 cup low-sodium chicken stock, homemade or prepared
2 tablespoons whole wheat flour

Directions for the Baked Chicken:
Preheat oven to 350°F. Set oven rack to middle position. Coat a low-sided roasting pan with cooking spray.

Place chicken breast-side up in pan and fill cavity with quartered onion. Rub chicken with a small amount of olive oil: on top and under skin of the bird. Place rosemary sprigs under the skin and sprinkle with Chinese five-spice powder. Bake chicken for about 2 hours (basting chicken periodically), or until the meat is cooked through and skin is golden brown. Check for safe temperature with meat thermometer prior to removing from oven.

Directions for the Cider—Morel Sauce:
While chicken is baking, prepare the sauce. In a small saucepan over medium-high heat, boil cider for about 40 minutes until reduced to 1/2 cup. Watch closely so liquid does not boil over; reduce heat if necessary.

While cider is boiling, place a sauté pan over medium heat and add 1 tablespoon of olive oil. Add the morels and sauté for about 5 minutes. Add minced shallots and continue to sauté until shallots are transparent, when completed, turn off heat and let cool.
In the saucepan containing the reduced cider, add 1/2 cup chicken stock and mix well. Place heat on medium-low.

In a measuring cup or small container, whisk together the 2 tablespoons of flour and the remaining chicken stock. Add this mixture slowly to the saucepan of reduced cider and chicken stock, stirring continuously until the mixture thickens to gravy consistency. Add the morel and shallot mixture and mix thoroughly.

Serve Cider–Morel Sauce with the Baked Rosemary Chicken.

This earthy dish is flavorful and healthy! Low in fat, the game, morels, and buckwheat noodles are a great combination. Serve with a crisp dark-green salad and some crusty garlic bread. Feel free to try different noodles or pasta with this unique entrée.

Buckwheat Noodles with Grilled Game Sausage and Tomato-Infused Morel Sauce

Directions:

Coat the grill with cooking spray. Preheat the grill.

Coat the inside of a medium-sized sauté pan with cooking spray and sauté morels for 9 minutes, stirring frequently. When cooked, remove from heat and cool enough to handle. Slice into rounds and set aside.

In a medium-sized saucepan, add morel liquid and half-and-half; over medium-high heat, bring to a boil (10–12 minutes). Add tomato paste and mix thoroughly. Continue to cook until mixture thickens (about 4 minutes). Reduce heat and add horseradish; continue to cook about 10 minutes, then add oregano and morels. Let simmer gently for about 5 minutes; set aside.

In a large pot, cook the noodles according to package directions. Keep them al dente (cooked but firm); drain well.

While the noodles are cooking, place the sausage on the grill and cook about 10 minutes on each side or until nicely browned (the time will depend on the type of meat you choose). When done, slice on the diagonal and prepare to assemble the dish.

Reheat sauce if necessary. In a large bowl, combine the noodles, morel–tomato sauce, and the sliced sausage. Toss lightly to mix all ingredients. Place the noodle–sausage mixture on a serving platter or in a serving bowl. Garnish with Parmigiano–Reggiano if desired. Serve warm.

Yield: 8 servings

Ingredients:

1 1/2 ounces dried morels, brushed, reconstituted, drained (liquid reserved)
Olive oil cooking spray
12 ounces Japanese buckwheat noodles (soba) or any favorite pasta or noodles
1 cup reserved mushroom liquid
1 cup fat-free half-and-half
1 can (6 ounces) tomato paste
3 tablespoons prepared horseradish (or to taste)
3 tablespoons fresh chopped oregano leaves
1/2 teaspoon sea salt
1 lb. wild game sausage (preferably bison, wild boar, or any low-fat game meat)
Shredded Parmigiano–Reggiano cheese for garnish (optional)

Braised Antelope Shanks Smothered with Morels

This recipe calls for antelope shanks (easily obtainable via the Internet), but if you want to use lamb, veal, or another type of game, feel free to substitute. Using wild game, though, ensures very low fat with no loss of flavor! Add a side of creamy mashed potatoes or any other creamy vegetable and a deep green fresh salad. You can make this a day ahead and serve the following day; if you choose to do it all in one day; you will have to start very early!

Yield: 4–6 servings

Ingredients:

3 ounces dried morels, brushed, reconstituted (with at least 3 cups of boiling water), and drained (liquid reserved)

3–4 tablespoons olive oil

5–6 pounds South Texas whole antelope shanks (1 lb. each), rinsed in cool water and patted dry

1 large sweet yellow onion, peeled and chopped (about 2 cups)

1 1/2 cups rough-chopped celery with leaves (about 6 ribs)

2 cups peeled and rough-chopped carrots (about 6 carrots)

2 cloves garlic, peeled and finely minced or grated

1 (28 ounce) can petite-diced tomatoes, well drained (retain juice for another use)

1 teaspoon peeled and finely grated fresh ginger root

1 hot finger pepper, seeded, deveined, and finely chopped (about 1 tablespoon)

2 dried bay leaves

2 sprigs of fresh rosemary, about 3 inches each

Directions:

Preheat oven to 350°F. Set oven rack to middle position.

In a large round Dutch oven with 3–4 tablespoons of olive oil, heat to hot over medium-high heat; add shanks (do not crowd: if the pan doesn't accommodate all the shanks, you may have to do this in batches). Brown the shanks well on all sides, 10–12 minutes; remove to frying pan and set aside.

Keep Dutch oven on stove with remaining oil (if more than about 2 tablespoons, remove additional, leaving all brown bits in the pan); add onions and cook over medium-high heat for 6–8 minutes. Add celery and carrots and cook an additional 5 minutes; add garlic and cook 1–2 minutes longer. Turn heat off and stir in tomatoes, ginger, bay leaves, and rosemary. Add back the shanks and any liquid collected in the frying pan to the Dutch oven; set aside momentarily.

In the same frying pan that held the shanks, add 2 cups of reserved morel liquid and heat to a boil, stirring to release any residue from the shanks. Turn off the heat and let cool slightly; add 1 to 1/2 cup of the chicken stock and mix. Pour liquid mixture over the shanks and vegetables in the Dutch oven; cover the pot and place in preheated oven. *Note:* The liquid should not cover the shanks completely.

Meanwhile, in the same frying pan, place the reconstituted morels and about 1 cup of the remaining liquid; cook over medium heat for 6–7 minutes, stirring frequently. Remove morels from any remaining liquid and set aside.

While shanks are cooking, baste periodically with liquid in the pan. About 1 1/4 hours into the cooking process, add cooked morels to the Dutch oven and return to oven. At the 2-hour point, check the meat for doneness; it should be totally cooked at 2 1/2 hours. *Note:* Timing will vary depending on meat choice and weight of shanks. Further, the morels will soak up a great deal of liquid. You will need to add at least 1/2 cup of reserved, chilled chicken stock; mix in gently.

If using the 2-day process, let cool slightly and refrigerate until ready to proceed. Skim off any visible fat.

3 cups reserved mushroom liquid, divided
2–2 1/2 cups low-sodium chicken stock, divided; 1 1/2 cups chilled
1/2 cup red wine
1 tablespoon cornstarch
1/4 teaspoon kosher salt (optional)

Special Equipment:
Extra-large round Dutch oven or very large ovenproof pot with lid (at least 8 quarts, preferably 12)
Large frying or sauté pan

About 30–35 minutes prior to serving, reheat in oven (300°F). If doing it all in one day, continue process.

When shanks are hot and ready to serve; remove each shank to a low bowl and add vegetables and morels to accompany the shank. Place pot (with remaining pan juice) on top of stove over medium heat; add red wine. Heat to boil.

In a small bowl or cup, add 1 tablespoon of cornstarch (or a bit more if necessary) to 1/2 cup chilled chicken stock (or possibly more); whisk to mix thoroughly. Add this chicken stock slurry to pan juice–red wine mixture, stirring until it becomes a gravy (or to desired consistency). Check seasonings and add salt only if necessary. Ladle gravy over shanks, vegetables, and morels. Serve with a large dollop of mashed potatoes added to each bowl.

Grilled Chicken and Morel Tikka

If you love Indian-influenced food, this will be a recipe you will want to add to your repertoire. You need to plan ahead for this entrée; the chicken needs to marinate overnight. It is mildly seasoned, but if you like it spicy, turn up the heat and add a bit more cayenne! Serve with coconut-flavored brown rice or some hot naan.

Yield: 6–8 servings

Ingredients for the Marinade:
1 1/4 cup plain low-fat yogurt
3 garlic cloves, peeled and minced
1 tablespoon peeled, finely grated
    fresh ginger
1 1/2 teaspoons ground cumin
1/4 teaspoon ground turmeric
1/4 teaspoon cayenne
1/4 teaspoon ground vindaloo spice
    or ground coriander
1/4 teaspoon ground cardamom

Ingredients for the Chicken:
3 chicken breasts, split (6), skin and
    fat removed, rinsed and patted
    dry
Olive oil cooking spray/olive oil

Special Equipment:
Grill or broiler (adjust times
    accordingly depending on heat
    source)

Note: This recipe contains almonds, so be alerted for those with nut allergies.

Directions for the Marinade:
In a large glass bowl (one that comes with a plastic lid is ideal), add the yogurt, garlic, ginger, cumin, turmeric, cayenne, vindaloo or coriander, and cardamom. Mix all ingredients thoroughly.

With a very sharp small knife, lightly slit each of the 6 pieces of chicken on the smooth side, making 3 slits per piece. Submerge pieces of chicken in the marinade, making sure all are equally covered. Cover the bowl with lid or with plastic wrap and refrigerate overnight, turning pieces over at least once.

Directions for the Chicken and Morels:
Coat grill grate well with cooking spray or dampen a paper towel with olive oil and wipe grate. Heat grill to medium.

Remove chicken from marinade, wiping off most of the yogurt base.

Place chicken on grill and cook for 15–17 minutes (this will depend on size of chicken breasts).

Coat tops of breasts with cooking spray or brush with olive oil and turn over onto grill. Cook another 15–17 minutes (or until meat reaches 150°F). Remove and let meat rest (temperature will rise a bit). *Note:* Remember that the meat will be cooked later in the sauce—don't overcook! When chicken is cool enough to handle, remove meat from bones and cut into 1-inch cubes; set aside.

While chicken is grilling, place almonds in a pan whose inside is coated with cooking spray and sauté over medium heat for 4–5 minutes; set aside to cool. Place almonds in a food processor bowl and process on pulse until finely ground; set aside.

In a large nonstick sauté pan whose insides are coated with cooking spray, sauté morels over medium heat for 6–8 minutes. Remove from heat and set aside.

In a large heavy casserole or round Dutch oven with lid, heat olive oil over medium-high heat; add the onions, garlic, and ginger, stirring occasionally, 8–9 minutes, or until lightly browned. Add the chili powder, cayenne, and garam masala; cook for an additional minute, or until fragrant. Add the canned tomatoes with juice, sugar, salt, and white pepper. Cover the pot and cook over medium heat, about 20 minutes, stirring occasionally. Add half-and-half and ground almonds. Reduce heat to low and cook sauce about 8 minutes, stirring occasionally.

To the simmering sauce, add the chicken and morels; simmer gently for an additional 8–10 minutes, stirring frequently. Serve with a coconut-flavored brown rice or piping-hot naan.

Ingredients for the Sauce:

2–2 1/2 cups fresh morels, wiped clean, quickly rinsed if necessary, drained and halved if large

1 1/2 tablespoons olive oil

1 large sweet yellow onion, peeled and finely chopped

3 cloves garlic, peeled and finely minced

1 1/2 finely grated fresh ginger

1 1/2 teaspoons chili powder

1/2–3/4 teaspoon cayenne (or more to taste)

1 3/4 teaspoons ground garam masala (see Addtional Tips, p. 127)

1 1/2 cans (42 ounces) petite-diced tomatoes, juice included

1/4–1/2 teaspoon kosher salt

1/8 teaspoon white pepper

1/2 teaspoon sugar or sugar substitute

1 1/2 cup fat-free half-and-half

3/4 cup raw almonds

Chicken, Bean, and Morel Stew

A warm and hearty one-dish meal, this can be served any time of the year! I usually reserve it for winter meals, but it is also perfect for any gray day, or if you just need some comfort food. Also great for dinner guests—serve with some very crusty rustic bread and a deep green salad.

Yield: 6 generous portions (8 smaller portions)

Ingredients:

2 ounces dried morels, brushed, reconstituted, and drained (at least 1 1/2 cups liquid reserved)

2 slices hickory smoked bacon, chopped and cooked, about 3 tablespoons.

1 large sweet yellow onion, peeled and chopped

2 cloves garlic, peeled and minced

1 small green sorrento pepper (mildly hot), seeded, deveined, and trimmed (any hot pepper of choice)

1 red sweet pepper, chopped (about 1 cup), seeded and deveined

1 large ripe tomato, cored and chopped

1/2 cup frozen spinach, thawed and squeezed dry (or equal of fresh cooked and drained)

3 1/2 cups cooked pinto beans or canned equivalent (if using canned, rinse and drain beans)

4 cups cooked white-meat chicken, cut into bite-sized pieces

1 cup lime-flavored light beer, or "lite" beer with juice of 1/2 lime added

1 cup reserved morel liquid

1 1/2 cups low-sodium chicken stock (have more on hand if later you want to thin the stew)

2 tablespoons fresh cilantro

1 teaspoon ground cumin

1/2 teaspoon sea salt

Tabasco® Sauce (optional)

Note: If you want your stew more of a soup consistency, add a bit more chicken stock at the end.

Directions:

In a large round Dutch oven, extra large saucepan, or pot, add morels and 1/2 cup of reserved liquid over medium heat for 6–8 minutes, stirring frequently. When morels have absorbed all liquid, remove from heat and cool slightly; finely chop morels in a food processor or with a knife; set aside.

In the same pan, cook the bacon over medium heat until crisp, 6–7 minutes; remove bacon and set aside. With the remaining bacon grease (use only 1—2 teaspoons) in the pan, add chopped onion and cook for 4 minutes or until lightly brown. Add the garlic and sauté for about 2 minutes; add both peppers, and continue to cook for about 5 minutes. Add tomatoes and cook an additional 3–4 minutes; mix in spinach, stirring until completely incorporated. Add in the reserved morels, drained beans, chicken, lime-flavored beer, morel liquid, low-sodium chicken stock, cilantro, cumin, and salt, stirring gently so as not to break up the beans. Reduce heat and simmer bean and morel mixture for about 25 minutes (adding more chicken stock if you want the stew thinner). At the 10-minute mark, add in the cooked bacon and cooked chicken and mix thoroughly; continue to heat until all is warmed throughout, 6–10 minutes.

Adjust seasoning and add a few drops of Tabasco® if desired. Serve in a low bowl with a side of crusty baguette right on the bowl.

A dramatic presentation for this salad—the long red peppers make for a great backdrop. Add assorted colored greens around the peppers for additional color and texture. You can also place the salad in a hollowed-out cucumber, melon, or tomato, or make into a wrap with a large lettuce leaf. Serve as an entrée or appetizer just by changing the container for the salad!

Chilled Crab and Morel Salad Mounded in Long Sweet Red Peppers

Directions:

In a medium-sized nonstick sauté pan over medium heat, cook morels with about 1/4 cup of reserved liquid (8–9 minutes), stirring frequently. Set aside to cool; when cool to the touch, slice morels into rounds and set aside.

Lay the red peppers down on a cutting board and cut out a canoe or diamond shape in the lateral side of the pepper (leaving green stem intact) going down toward the end, making an opening for the salad filling. Seed and devein the peppers; set aside.

In a saucepan fitted with a collapsible steamer and lid in place, add water and steam the asparagus over medium-high heat, 8–9 minutes (or steam it in any way you choose). Remove asparagus from steamer and let cool; set aside.

In a medium-sized bowl, add crabmeat, celery, morel rounds, and lemon juice; toss to mix thoroughly. Set aside.

In a food processor, process cooked asparagus, mayonnaise, yogurt, scallions and salt. When completely processed and smooth, pour over crabmeat and morel mixture; toss lightly and thoroughly with a spatula. Adjust seasoning, if necessary. Chill for at least an hour.

Mound the crab and morel mixture into the opening of the pepper and serve.

Yield: 6 servings

Ingredients:

1 1/2 ounces dried morels, brushed, reconstituted, and drained (liquid reserved)

6 whole "ancient" long sweet red peppers, rinsed well.

8 ounces fresh asparagus, trimmed

16 ounces crabmeat (premium lump—fully cooked), drained and rinsed

2 ribs celery, trimmed, cut lengthwise and finely sliced (about 1 cup)

1 tablespoon freshly squeezed lemon juice

1/4 cup low-fat mayonnaise, homemade or prepared

1/4 cup heavy yogurt (Laban; see Additional Tips, p. 125)

2 scallions (green and white part), rinsed, trimmed, and cut into pieces

1/8 teaspoon kosher salt

Crawfish Étouffée Loaded with Morels

This is a perfect dinner or luncheon entrée—and great for a party. Wonderful to make this when the herbs are in full bloom, though you can also use dried herbs; be sure to adjust amounts accordingly. If you like étouffée, you will love this with the morels! Instead of 2 pounds of crayfish, the morels fill the bill for 1 pound! Whatever you don't eat you can freeze for up to three months.

Yield: Big batch (12 servings)

Ingredients:
Olive oil cooking spray
4 ounces dried morels, brushed, reconstituted, and drained (liquid reserved)
2 tablespoons olive oil
1–2 two sweet yellow onions, peeled and diced small (about 4 cups)
8 ribs celery with leaves, trimmed (leaves retained) and sliced (about 4 cups)
4 cups sliced okra (or 16-ounce bag frozen okra, thawed)
3 cloves garlic, peeled and minced
2 cans petite-diced tomatoes (28 ounces each), juice included
1 bottle (3 cups) white wine, preferably a Chardonnay
3 cups low-sodium seafood stock (homemade or prepared) or you can use clam juice if you don't have seafood stock
1 tablespoon fresh tarragon, chopped
1 tablespoon fresh lemon verbena, chopped (or 2 teaspoons lemon zest)

3 tablespoons fresh parsley, finely chopped
1 pound crawfish tail meat, fully cooked, peeled, and deveined
2 teaspoons spicy Tabasco® Worcestershire
Sea salt (if necessary, depending on saltiness of stock)

Tabasco® or red pepper sauce to taste

Special Equipment: Whatever type of pot or Dutch oven you use, make sure it will accommodate at least 6 quarts.

Directions:
In a large nonstick sauté pan coated inside with cooking spray, over medium heat, cook reconstituted morels in 1/2 cup reserved morel liquid for 5–6 minutes; set aside to cool. When cool enough to handle, halve the morels lengthwise and set aside.

In a large round Dutch oven, extra-large saucepan, or stockpot, over medium-high heat, add olive oil; when oil is hot, add onion and cook until lightly browned, 8–10 minutes. Reduce heat to medium and add celery; cook for 5 minutes. Add okra; sauté for 4 minutes; add garlic and tomatoes (including juice) and stir. Let mixture incorporate for about 5 minutes before adding anything else.
Add wine and seafood stock; bring to a boil. Add tarragon, lemon verbena (zest), and parsley; stir to mix all ingredients thoroughly. Reduce heat to simmer and continue to cook for 45 minutes.

Add crawfish tail meat, reserved cooked morels, Tabasco® Worcestershire, and allow mixture to meld, about 10 minutes. Season Étouffée with salt if necessary; add Tabasco® to taste. Serve with fluffy brown rice (at least 1/2 cup cooked rice per person) and a large crisp green salad dressed with a lemon vinaigrette.

These tostadas are flavorful and filling! No sauce needed; it's all in the entrée. While many traditional tostadas have cheese, these do not; they are light and healthy and full of flavor. They can also be used as an appetizer.

Duck and Morel Tostadas with Napa Coleslaw and Guacamole

Directions:

Coat grill grate with olive oil cooking spray or dampen a paper towel with olive oil and wipe grate. Preheat grill to medium-high.

Trim any excess fat from duck breasts, then place them, skin side down, on grill. Sear until nicely browned and marked with grill marks (4–5 minutes). Turn down grill to medium and turn over duck to cook other side (about 3 minutes). Check duck breasts to make sure they are not cooking too fast. Cook an additional 3–4 minutes or until desired doneness. Let rest; when cool enough to handle, remove skin and slice thinly (about 1 1/2 cups). Place in a bowl and set aside.

In a medium-sized nonstick sauté pan, add reconstituted morels and 1/4 cup of reserved liquid; cook over medium-high heat for 8–9 minutes (adding more liquid if necessary during cooking process), stirring frequently. When morels have absorbed almost all liquid, remove from heat and cool slightly. Cut the morels in half lengthwise and add to the bowl of duck slices; add 2 tablespoons of the adobo sauce from the can; set aside.

In a medium-sized bowl, combine napa cabbage, cilantro, chives, chipotles, lime juice, and seasoned rice vinegar. Mix well and set aside.

In a large heavy skillet coated with cooking spray, pan fry tortillas if they are homemade or bake on a baking sheet if prepared.

Divide all of the ingredients into 6 equal portions; assemble each tostada by topping each tortilla with duck–morel mixture, napa cabbage coleslaw, and top with a dollop of guacamole. Top with additional cooked morel halves if desired. Serve with some low-fat refried beans and a small side of rice.

Yield: 6 tostadas

Ingredients:

1 ounce dried morels, brushed, reconstituted, and drained (liquid reserved) (add more morels for optional topping)

2 (6-ounce) duck breast halves with skin on topside (frozen raw duck breasts are available in packages of 2)

Olive oil cooking spray/olive oil

3 cups rinsed, thinly sliced, and chopped napa cabbage

1/2 cup cilantro, stems removed, rinsed, and dried, then chopped

2 tablespoons finely chopped chives

Canned chipotles in adobo: 2 peppers chopped and 2 tablespoons of sauce; separate peppers from sauce

1 1/2 tablespoons lime juice (juice from one lime)

2 tablespoons seasoned rice vinegar

6 small corn tortillas (see Additional Tips, p. 130, on making tortillas)

1/2 cup guacamole

Grilled and Skewered Morel–Bison Kafta

This ethnic-inspired skewered entrée is Middle Eastern in flavor, using morels and bison meat to make a unique main dish that is low in fat and calories. Serve with rice pilaf and roasted vegetables. Add a warm piece of pita bread for those who want a wrap. You can prepare a side of thick yogurt flavored with onion for those who crave a side sauce.

Yield: 14 skewers (you can easily cut recipe in half, or just freeze extras for quick dinners)

Ingredients:

2 1/2 ounces dried morels, brushed, reconstituted, and drained (liquid reserved)
Olive oil cooking spray/olive oil
3 pounds ground bison meat (you can use ground beef, lamb, or any ground game meat)
1 1/2 cups peeled sweet yellow onion, finely chopped
1 tablespoon ground cumin
2 teaspoons ground cardamom
1 teaspoon allspice
1/2 teaspoon cayenne
1 1/2 teaspoons kosher or sea salt
2 cups chopped curly parsley (*Note:* if using a food processor, chop on pulse)

Special Equipment:

Thick bamboo 12-inch skewers
48 mm scoop (optional, to keep the balls of meat uniform in size)
Barbecue Grill

Note: If using bamboo skewers on the grill, soak skewers in water overnight prior to use.

Directions:

Coat the inside of a large nonstick sauté pan with cooking spray and place on medium heat; add the morels. Cook for 8–9 minutes, stirring frequently. Set aside to cool. Once cool enough to handle, process in a food processor or chop finely with a knife. Set aside.

Generously spray grill rack with cooking spray or dampen a paper towel with olive oil and wipe grate. Preheat grill to medium.

In a large bowl, combine the bison meat, onion, cumin, cardamom, allspice, cayenne, salt, parsley, and chopped morels. Mix well with hands to evenly disperse all of the ingredients.

Remove one skewer at a time from the water; wipe off. With the scoop or by hand, form a small golf-sized ball out of the mixture. Roll the mixture into a perfect balls. Push the skewer through the middle of the kafta meatball. Repeat until you have five kafta meatballs on each skewer.

When all skewers are loaded with kafta orbs, place on prepared grill and cover with lid. Cook for about 10 minutes (5–6 minutes on each side until nicely browned with grill marks), or to desired doneness. Remove cooked kafta from the grill and serve. Don't overcook these—remember the bison has negligible fat.

David McCall Johnston

Elegant Vegetable-Morel Stuffed Brisket

This elegant brisket is pretty as well as flavorful. Loaded with vegetables, morels, and chestnuts, it is a great way to get everyone (including the kids) to eat a portion of their veggies. Serve with fluffy mashed potatoes, roasted red potatoes, or even yams. A hearty meal for family and special enough to serve to dinner guests!

Yield: 6–8 servings

Ingredients for the Meat:

4 3/4–5 pound brisket of beef, fat trimmed (leave some fat on the bottom side), and a good-sized pocket cut (have the butcher do this for you)

Freshly ground sea salt

Freshly ground black pepper

3 tablespoons olive oil

2 leeks, white and light green part only, cut in half and washed thoroughly

Bottle of medium to dry red wine

Directions:

Preheat oven to 400°F. Place oven rack to the middle position.

In a low ovenproof dish or pan whose inside is coated with cooking spray, add the garlic bulb, julienne-cut carrots, sliced leeks, and chestnut halves; bake for 30 minutes (or until cloves of garlic feel soft). Remove from oven.

When cloves of garlic are cool enough to handle, remove the cloves from the skin; set aside. At the same time, let brisket come to almost room temperature, then rinse well under cool water. Pat meat dry with paper toweling; lightly salt and pepper all sides of the brisket.

Coat the inside of a large nonstick sauté pan with cooking spray and cook the morels in it over medium heat for about 6 minutes, adding 1/4–1/2 cup of the reserved morel liquid. Set aside.
Reduce oven temperature to 325°F.

In a large Dutch oven or ovenproof pan, add the 3 tablespoons of olive oil and place over medium-high heat on stove—when hot, add meat and brown on all sides; remove from heat source.

Put the browned meat on a flat surface and place the roasted vegetables, chestnuts, and morels in the pocket, pushing the stuffing all the way into the pocket; make sure the pocket is well packed. Place the stuffed brisket back into the Dutch oven. Place the browned garlic cloves and nonroasted leeks all around the brisket. Pour red wine over the meat, garlic, and leeks (wine should be 1 1/2 inches–2 inches deep—don't use it all). Cover the pot and place in the oven.

Cook for about three hours; check occasionally, and baste. Add more red wine if necessary or desired. When meat is cooked and fork tender, turn off oven and let sit for approximately 15 minutes. Remove the meat to a platter or cutting board. Cut the brisket going across the grain into thick slices. The slices will appear to have a stuffed section in the middle. Spoon off the layer of fat from the juices in the pan, the drizzle some of the pan juice over the meat and serve.

Ingredients for the Stuffing:

2 ounces dried morels, brushed, reconstituted, and drained (liquid reserved)

Olive oil cooking spray

1 head garlic, left whole and coated with olive oil cooking spray

4 carrots (use the tender ones with the green tops), washed, tops removed, and julienne cut.

1 large leek (white and light green part only), sliced in half, then quartered and washed thoroughly

2 1/2–3 cups peeled and halved chestnuts

Special Equipment:

Large Dutch oven or any ovenproof pan with a lid that will accommodate your meat

Lobster and Morel Rolls

A bit of Cape Cod from your own kitchen! The lobster–morel salad is a twist on traditional lobster rolls that are found in the Northeast and usually contain chunks of lobster meat and mayonnaise; the addition of morels adds great flavor and texture. The tarragon bread rolls make this entrée really special, but if you don't have time to make your own, feel free to put the lobster—morel mixture onto low-fat hot dog buns that have been grilled or toasted on the exterior.

Yield: 8 Lobster and Morel Rolls (or maybe more depending on size of bread rolls)

Ingredients for the Rolls:
1 1/4 cups whole wheat flour
2 1/4–2 1/2 cups bread flour
1 3/4 teaspoons sea salt
2 1/2 teaspoons fast-rise yeast
1 tablespoon fresh tarragon or 1 teaspoon dried (more if desired)
3/4 cup fat-free half-and-half
2/3 cup water
3 tablespoons olive oil, plus more for oiling bowl and pan
2 tablespoons honey (preferably raw)
1 egg plus 1 tablespoon of cold water, beaten (egg wash)
1/8–1/4 cup butter substitute (for buttering outside of rolls, about 1 1/2 teaspoon each)

Special Equipment:
Instant-read thermometer
Glass bowl
Plastic wrap
Bread pan/loaf pan 9 1/2 × 5 1/2 × 2 3/4 inches (or a similar size)
Pastry brush

Directions:
Preheat oven to 350°F. Place oven rack to middle position.

Lightly oil a glass bowl (for letting the dough rise); set aside.

Lightly flour a flat surface to knead dough; have this ready when dough comes out of food processor.

In the bowl of a food processor, add whole wheat flour and 2 1/4 cups bread flour, yeast, tarragon, and salt; process slightly; leave in place. *Note:* This step can be done without the use of a food processor; it just takes more time if you mix this in a bowl with a wooden spoon.

In a medium-sized saucepan over medium-low heat, add half-and-half, water, honey, and olive oil; heat to 120–124°F. Pour into the flour mixture in the food processor and process on pulse until a ball forms. Check the dough; if seems sticky, add up to 1/4 cup more bread flour and reprocess. When the dough ball appears on top of the blade, remove to floured surface.

Knead until smooth and elastic, 2–3 minutes.

Place dough ball into oiled glass bowl and cover with plastic wrap. Let rise in a warm area, free from drafts, for 45–60 minutes, or until dough has doubled in size.

Punch dough down and remove from bowl to floured surface; roll out to an even rectangle (about 10 inches); and roll the dough up, sealing the bottom and the ends by turning it over and placing it back in the bowl and covering it with plastic wrap to double in size again, about 30 more minutes.

While dough is rising, cook the lobster (see Additional Tips for cooking lobster, p. 131).

Place the dough in a well-oiled bread pan; let rise 15 minutes then coat top with egg wash. Place in oven and bake for about 40 minutes (turning pan at 20 minutes for even browning). Remove bread from oven when nicely browned; cool for 15–20 minutes in pan; and let sit on rack for at least 1 hour to cool completely before slicing it into "Texas Toast"-sized slices (about 1/2 inch thick).

Coat the inside of a large nonstick sauté pan with cooking spray and gently sauté the fresh morels over medium heat for 6–8 minutes, making sure the mushrooms are cooked through; set aside to cool.

In a large bowl, add the lobster meat, cooked morels, mayonnaise, and salt; mix well. Taste and adjust seasoning if necessary.

Assembly:
Lightly grill or pan-fry in a nonstick sauté pan each slice of toast, on one side only (butter-side down). Gently fold each slice in half, keeping soft side on the interior; add lettuce (optional) and fill with about 1/2 cup of lobster–morel filling. Serve with a side of assorted raw veggies.

Ingredients for the Lobster–Morel Filling:

3/4 pound fresh morels, brushed, lightly rinsed, patted dry, and halved lengthwise; if small, keep them whole (if using dried morels in place of fresh, you will need at least 3 cups cooked)

Olive oil cooking spray

1 pound live lobster, about 3 1/2 lbs., cooked, meat removed (about 3 1/2 cups meat), rough chopped, and chilled (or 3 1/2 cups of purchased lobster meat)

3/4 cup fat-free mayonnaise (homemade or prepared)

1/2 teaspoon sea salt

Assorted greens of your choice (a mix of lettuce) to line rolls (optional)

Hearty Crockpot Stew with Morels

This hearty stew is great anytime of the year; use dried morels as you need the liquid from reconstituting those prized fungi. It has a nice morel flavor! Serve with some fluffy mashed potatoes and a crisp green salad, or skip the potatoes and serve in a bread bowl: hollow out a round bread and place the finished stew inside for serving; use one large or 4–6 small individual rounds.

Yield: 4–6 servings

Ingredients:

2 pounds bison or piedmontese beef stew meat, trimmed and cut into bite-sized pieces

3 ounces dried morels, brushed and reconstituted (at least 2 1/2 cups liquid reserved)

1 bunch carrots (about 8 carrots), peeled and cut into bite-sized pieces

1 bunch celery with leaves cut into bite-sized pieces

2 medium-sized sweet yellow onions, peeled and cubed

3/4 pound fresh okra, trimmed, rinsed, and cut into bite-sized pieces

1 can (28 ounces) petite-diced tomatoes, including juice

2 1/2 cups reserved morel liquid

1 cup red wine

3 tablespoons quick-cooking tapioca

2 teaspoons kosher or sea salt

2 sprigs fresh rosemary, about 2 inches each

Special Equipment:

large crockpot

Directions:

In a medium-sized nonstick sauté pan over medium heat, brown the meat until all sides are well browned; remove from heat and place meat in a crockpot ceramic insert.

In the same sauté pan, cook the morels using about 1/4 cup morel liquid; cook and stir (about 7 minutes and the liquid is absorbed). When morels are cool enough to handle, slice in half lengthwise (if very large, cut into quarters). Add morels slices to the crockpot.

Add carrots, celery, onion, okra, tomatoes, 2 1/2 cups reserved morel liquid, red wine, tapioca, salt, and rosemary. Stir all ingredients until well mixed. Cover the crockpot and set to high.

Cook the stew for 7–8 hours, or until the meat is tender. Stir stew occasionally and check seasonings. Remove from heat and serve.

This light and fluffy omelet is perfect for breakfast, brunch, lunch, or dinner. What could be a better filling? Serve with a crisp green salad with fruit and a potato accompaniment or a small homemade muffin.

Morel, Scallion, and Spinach Omelet

Directions:

Coat a 9 1/2-inch nonstick frying pan (with oven-proof handle) with cooking spray.

Sauté the morels for about 4 minutes over medium heat and add scallion; continue to sauté until scallion is wilted. Remove morels and scallion; let cool slightly and slice morels into rounds; set aside.

In a large bowl, whisk together the 4 whole eggs and 3 egg whites along with the light coconut milk and sea salt until light and frothy; set aside momentarily.

Preheat oven to 400°F. Set oven rack to middle position.

Wipe out sauté pan. Coat inside of pan with olive oil cooking spray and heat over medium heat; when oil starts to bubble, pour in egg mixture.

Let egg mixture cook for 6–7 minutes; add shredded cheese to half of the cooking eggs; cook about 2 more minutes. Add the morel–scallion mixture to the cheese half of the eggs. Top with the raw fresh baby spinach and cook until bottom of egg is lightly brown.

Place the sauté pan in the oven for about 15 minutes, or until the plain side of the egg is fully cooked. Remove pan from oven and fold the plain side of the omelet over the filled side. Place a large serving plate over the pan and flip it over to plate the omelet. Serve with a sprinkling of chopped morels and scallions, if desired.

Yield: 2–4 servings (depending on portion)

Ingredients:
Olive oil cooking spray
1 ounce dried morels, brushed, reconstituted, and drained (liquid reserved for future use)
1/4–1/2 cup chopped scallions (green part only)
4 whole eggs plus 3 egg whites (3 yolks reserved for another recipe or cooked for your pets)
1/2 cup light coconut milk
1/4 teaspoon sea salt
1/2 cup shredded light cheese (or Dubliner Irish Cheese)
1 brimming cup of fresh baby spinach, washed, rinsed, and dried

Morel, Vegetable, and Meat Pie

Reminiscent of a loose burger, this open-faced meat pie has a loose vegetable and mushroom interior with a crispy crust. A great entrée for a cool fall lunch or dinner, but it would be good any time of the year!) The best container for baking this dish is a very low ovenproof bowl that will accommodate 6 cups of filling.

Yield: 4–6 servings

Ingredients:

1 1/2 ounces dried morels, brushed, reconstituted, and drained (liquid reserved)

1 9-inch pie crust (homemade or prepared)

1 pound ground grass-fed beef, bison, or antelope (any lean meat)

Olive oil cooking spray

2 red onions, peeled and finely chopped

1 cup peeled, shredded carrot

2 tablespoons olive oil

1 cup peeled, shredded baking potato

2 tablespoons whole wheat flour

1 cup low-sodium beef stock (homemade or prepared)

1/2 teaspoon salt (depending on saltiness of stock)

2 tablespoons fresh flat-leaf parsley, chopped

Directions:

Preheat oven to 350°F. Set oven rack to middle position.

Coat inside of baking dish with cooking spray.

In a medium-sized nonstick sauté pan, add reconstituted morels and 1/4–1/2 cup of reserved liquid; cook over medium heat for about 6 minutes, stirring frequently. When morels have absorbed almost all of the liquid, remove from heat and cool slightly; finely chop morels in a food processor or with a knife. Set aside in a medium-large bowl.

In the same pan, lightly brown ground meat over medium heat; drain any fat (it should be negligible). Stir to brown evenly (6–8 minutes); when cooked, remove to bowl with morels.

Coat the same pan with cooking spray if needed; sauté the onions for 3–5 minutes or just until they begin to brown. Add shredded carrot and continue to cook for about 4 minutes, stirring frequently. Remove from pan and set aside in bowl with the meat and morels.

In the same pan, add 2 tablespoons of olive oil and heat. At the same time, toss shredded potato with the flour and add to the hot pan of oil; stir constantly making sure to scrape the pan gently to get up the bulk of the browned bits (about 4 minutes). Remove the potatoes to the bowl containing all of the other ingredients; mix well.

Deglaze the hot pan from the potatoes with the beef stock; continue to cook for 8 minutes or until liquid has reduced by half. Add the reduced stock and pan bits to the bowl with the other ingredients; mix well. Add salt (if necessary) and fresh parsley; mix thoroughly.

Place the piecrust in the center of the sprayed baking dish, fitting it to the sides (you should have 1 1/4 inch of overhang); gently flute the edges. Add the filling to the piecrust (6 cups); fold the fluted edges over the morel/meat filling (the center will not be covered). Top the filling with the circle of aluminum foil to keep it from drying out.

Bake the open-faced pie in the oven for 1 hour and 10 to 1 hour and fifteen minutes, or until crust is crisp and lightly brown. About 40 minutes into the cooking process, remove foil circle and continue to bake; check at the 60-minute mark for doneness. *Note:* If at any point exposed meat area seems to be drying out, re-place foil circle.

When fully baked, remove pie from oven and let sit on a trivet or hot pad for 10–12 minutes prior to serving.

Special Equipment:
Round baking dish 8 inches in diameter (1 3/4 inches in height (or any baking dish of similar size)
Round piece of aluminum foil to fit inside of meat pie (this will cover the morel/meat filling)

Note: Using an angled pie server will make it easier to serve—remember, the inside is loose! Serve with steamed green vegetables or a big salad.

Morel and Artichoke Heart Lasagna

This is great for a lunch or dinner entrée—and can be made all year round thanks to dried morels and frozen artichoke hearts! Perfect for entertaining or just for the family. A fun project for the kids is to have them help sort out the layers. Use lasagna noodles of your choice; I have used homemade spinach noodles, semolina noodles, and even organic brown rice Lasagna noodles to make this dish gluten free. For Homemade Spinach Pasta, see Additional Tips, p. 128.

Yield: 8–12 servings

Ingredients:

3 ounces dried morels, or a combination of 1 1/2 ounces morels and 1 1/2 ounces trompettes, brushed, reconstituted, and drained (at least 1/2 cup liquid reserved)

1 package frozen artichoke hearts, 12 ounces, thawed, chopped, and drained (if fresh about 3 cups)

Olive oil cooking spray

1 leek, white and light green part only (about 1 cup), rinsed, thinly sliced and rerinsed

1/2 cup plus 2 tablespoons Mirin (sweet Asian cooking wine), divided

1 (10 ounce) package lasagna noodles

3 cups ricotta (homemade or prepared)

2 cloves garlic, peeled and finely minced

2–3 eggs (or 4–5 egg whites)

Directions:

Preheat oven to 350°F. Place oven rack to middle position. Coat inside of lasagna pan generously with cooking spray and set aside.

In a nonstick medium-sized sauté pan whose insides are coated with cooking spray, sauté reconstituted mushrooms with 1/2 cup of mushroom liquid over medium-high heat for 6–8 minutes; set aside to cool slightly. Remove mushrooms from pan to a medium-large bowl and set aside. Add artichokes. In the same pan, sauté the leeks for about 3 minutes over medium heat; splash with 1–2 tablespoons Mirin. Mix well and remove leeks; place in same bowl with morels and artichokes and set aside. *Note:* Do not wash sauté pan; you will be using it for the cream sauce; you want those clinging flavors. When mixture cools a bit, process mushrooms, artichokes, and leeks on pulse in a food processor; set aside.

In a large stockpot or saucepan, cook lasagna noodles according to package directions; drain well and set aside. While noodles are cooking, combine ricotta, garlic, and eggs (or egg whites) in a medium-sized bowl; mix thoroughly and set aside.

In the sauté pan used for the morels and leeks, heat 3 tablespoons olive oil over medium heat and add the flour, whisking to incorporate; continue to heat and whisk until mixture is bubbly. Gradually add in the warmed half-and-half; continue whisking until thick. When all half-and-half is incorporated, add Mirin while continuing to whisk, about 2 minutes (sauce should be thickened, but not too thick).

Remove cream sauce from the heat and add to the morel and artichoke mixture; combine well. Taste and adjust seasoning (add salt if necessary). The consistency should be similar to a traditional meat sauce.

David McCall Johnston

3 tablespoons olive oil

3 tablespoons all-purpose flour or rice flour

2–3 tablespoons finely chopped fresh basil

1 cup fat-free half-and-half, slightly warmed

4 ounces part-skim mozzarella cheese, shredded

1/2 teaspoon kosher salt (if necessary)

Special Equipment:
Wire whisk
Lasagna pan, 9 × 13 inches

To assemble the lasagna: In lasagna pan coated with cooking spray, place a thin layer of the mushroom/artichoke sauce; top with a layer of lasagna noodles. Add a layer of sauce; add a layer of the ricotta mixture; sprinkle with some shredded mozzarella. Repeat process with the noodle layer and the rest of the ingredients in the same order. (There should be about 4 layers, depending on size of pan chosen.) When ready for the last layer, save a little extra sauce and mozzarella for the very top.

Bake for 30–45 minutes or until heated through. Remove from the oven and let rest for at least 10 minutes before serving. Accompany it with a crisp Italian-flavored deep-green salad and some sliced tomatoes.

Morel, Ramp, and Fiddlehead Fern Bread Pudding

This bread pudding is great for breakfast, brunch, lunch, or dinner. If serving for a meal other than breakfast, serve with a crisp green salad laden with fresh seasonal fruit. If making this out of spring season, substitute asparagus spears for fiddleheads.

Yield: 6–8 servings

Ingredients:
Olive oil cooking spray
1/4 cup olive oil
6 cups cubed soft Italian bread (1-inch cubes)
2 tablespoons low-calorie butter substitute
6 ounces fresh morels, brushed or rinsed and sliced into rounds
8 fresh ramps (wild leeks)—white bulb and purple part only, washed and sliced into narrow rounds
18–24 fiddlehead ferns (or 8 stalks fresh asparagus)
1/2 cup fat-free half-and-half
6 large eggs (if using only egg whites, use 10)
3/4 cup freshly grated Parmigiano–Reggiano cheese
Sea salt (1/4 teaspoon or to taste—remember the cheese contains salt)

Special Equipment:
1 baking pan (7 cups) and 1 baking sheet with sides

Directions:
Preheat oven to 400°F. Set oven rack set to middle position.

Coat baking pan and baking sheet with olive oil spray; set aside.

In a large bowl, toss bread cubes with olive oil. Place oiled cubes on a baking sheet and bake until golden brown and crisp (about 20 minutes).

Reduce oven temperature to 350°F.

In a medium-large nonstick sauté pan over medium-low heat, melt butter substitute. Add rounds of morels and cook for approximately 6 minutes (there will be some moisture). Stir to cook morels evenly.

Add the cut rounds of ramps and sauté mixture for about 3 minutes, or until transparent.

Add the fiddlehead ferns and cook for about a minute, just to cook lightly. Let mixture cool slightly.
Add toasted bread cubes to ramp mixture and toss until well mixed, set aside.

In a large bowl, whisk together half-and-half, eggs, and sea salt; add cheese.

Place mixture of toasted bread cubes in the well-sprayed baking pan. Pour egg mixture over bread cubes.

Bake approximately 45 minutes or until firm to the touch, golden brown in color, and crisp on top. Remove from oven and serve warm.

Earthy and scrumptious, this morel-sauced rabbit over farro and lentils is hearty and unique. The morels add a wonderful taste and texture to this dish. You can also replace the farro with rice or noodles—feel free to experiment with the starch below your protein!

Morel-Sauced Rabbit on a Bed of Farro and Lentils

Directions for Cooking Rabbit:

Lightly salt each piece of rabbit.

In a large heavy casserole (with a lid), over medium-high, heat the olive oil. Cook each piece of salted rabbit in the hot olive oil until nicely browned on all sides, 20–30 minutes. As each piece is browned, transfer to paper towels and let drain of any excess oil. When all pieces are removed from the pan, reduce heat to medium and add morel halves; cook for about 4 minutes. Add the shallots and continue to cook until lightly browned. There shouldn't be any remaining oil, if there is, remove carefully with a baster. Don't remove shallots or browned bits; discard oil only.

Transfer the rabbit back to the casserole, add morels, and add enough chicken stock just to cover all of the meat and mushrooms.

Add mustard to taste (usually about 1/3 of a large jar); mix into the stock. Cover the pot. Bring the chicken stock to a boil and reduce to simmer. Continue to cook for approximately 1 1/2 hours, or until the meat is very tender.

While rabbit is cooking, make farro in a rice cooker or in a pot according to package directions. At the same time, cook the lentils in a separate pot according to package directions, until no water remains. Once farro and lentils are cooked, toss together with fresh minced parsley (if desired). Serve the cooked rabbit and morels over the farro and lentils and offer extra pan liquid on the table for sauce enthusiasts.

Yield: 8 servings

Ingredients for the Rabbit:
2 rabbits, 3–4 pounds, each cut into 6 pieces, all fat removed, rinsed, and patted dry
1 teaspoon kosher salt
1/4 cup olive oil (or a slight bit more if necessary)
Chicken stock (homemade or prepared), enough to cover the rabbit (6–8 cups)
Coarse-seeded mustard, to taste
8 ounces fresh morels, brushed or lightly rinsed and halved lengthwise
3 tablespoons shallots, peeled and minced

Ingredients for the Farro and Lentils:
2 cups farro, cooked in a rice cooker or in a pot according to package instructions
1 cup black (beluga) lentils, rinsed, picked over for stones, and cooked according to package directions
1/2 cup fresh flat-leaf parsley, rinsed and finely chopped (optional)

Morel, Crab, Ramp, and Fiddlehead Fern Strudel

This elegant strudel is crisp and filled with spring splendor. If you make this during another season, substitute asparagus for the fiddleheads, and leeks (white and light green part only) for the ramps. Great served for brunch, lunch, or dinner, this dish works beautifully for a buffet table, sit-down dinner party, or luncheon.

Yield: 8 dinner-sized servings

Ingredients:

Olive oil cooking spray

2 ounces dried morels, brushed, reconstituted, and drained (reserve 2 1/4 cups liquid, divided)

1 cup sliced ramps (about 16, depending on size), white and purple part only

1/4 cup spiced rum

2 cups fiddlehead ferns, steamed or sautéed (or substitute equal amount of chopped asparagus)

16 ounces crabmeat (premium lump, fully cooked), drained and rinsed

4 tablespoons low-calorie butter substitute

4 tablespoons all-purpose flour

2 teaspoons crab base (homemade or prepared—Minor's has a great one)

2 cups fat-free half-and-half

2 teaspoons fresh finely chopped rosemary

1/8 teaspoon white pepper

1 package of fillo (phyllo) dough (9 × 14), prepared (you won't need the full package)

Directions:

Preheat oven to 350°F. Place oven rack to middle position.

In a large nonstick sauté pan coated with cooking spray, cook morels with 1/4 cup reserved morel liquid over medium heat, for 6–8 minutes. Add ramps and continue to sauté for another 4 minutes. Add rum, cook about 2 minutes, and set aside. When cool, process on pulse in a food processor to a rough chop.

In a glass bowl or large measuring cup, add 2 cups of the morel liquid; stir in the crab base until it dissolves; set aside.

In a medium-sized saucepan, melt butter substitute over medium heat; whisk in flour and cook until paste consistency and bubbly. Slowly add half-and-half, whisking continuously; add in reserved morel–crab liquid and continue stirring until mixture appears thickened, smooth, and coats the back of a spoon, about 20 minutes. When mixture reaches correct consistency, add rosemary and white pepper. Add the crabmeat, fiddleheads, and chopped morel mixture; set aside momentarily.

Coat the baking pan generously with cooking spray; cover with one sheet of fillo dough, which is fragile, so take care not to rip the sheet. Coat the sheet and add 2 more sheets (don't spray in between).

Add 1/3 of the morel/crab cream mixture; repeat process. When you have 3 layers, top with 5–6 layers of fillo dough; spraying lightly between layers and on the top. Place in oven and bake 1 hour or until sauce appears bubbly and top fillo layer is browned and crisp.

Let rest slightly before cutting into servings. Serve strudel with a big salad of greens and a garnish of seasonal fruit.

Special Equipment: 14 × 10 × 2 1/2 inch (or similar size) rectangular ovenproof baking pan

This recipe calls for morels and trompette mushrooms, but feel free to use all morels or any combination of wild mushrooms. The intensity of flavor in this particular version comes from the combination of morels and trompettes. The moist and flavorful meatloaf is delicious enough for the most elegant company—NO KETCHUP! Serve with mashed potatoes and a crisp green salad.

Sumptuous Morel, Trompette, and Turkey Meatloaf

Directions:

Preheat the oven to 350°F. Set oven rack to middle position. Coat loaf pan with cooking spray.

In a large nonstick sauté pan, add 1 1/2 tablespoons olive oil and sauté the chopped shallots until lightly brown (about 3 minutes). Remove shallots from pan to cool. Add the remaining tablespoon of olive oil and repeat the process with the mushrooms, cooking about 9 minutes and adding 3–4 tablespoons of the reserved liquid to the pan; stir occasionally. Set aside; when cool, process on pulse in a food processor or rough chop.

In a large bowl, add the cooked and chopped mushrooms, chopped shallots, garlic, turkey meat, bread crumbs, eggs or egg whites, lime juice, maple syrup, salt, and cayenne; mix thoroughly.

Place meatloaf mixture in loaf pan and set in oven. While baking, if meat appears dry on top, brush with a small amount of olive oil or spray. Bake for about 60 minutes until lightly brown on top (or internally 165–170°F on an instant read thermometer).

Before serving, remove any excess liquid with a baster or carefully tilt to release (if using all white-meat turkey, there should be virtually no liquid).

Yield: 6–8 servings

Ingredients:

Olive oil cooking spray
2 ounces dried mushrooms (1 ounce morels, 1 ounce black trompettes), brushed and reconstituted (liquid reserved)
2 1/2 tablespoons olive oil, divided
1 cup peeled, finely chopped shallots
2 cloves garlic, peeled and minced
1 1/2 pounds ground raw white-meat turkey
1 1/4 cups Italian-flavored bread crumbs seasoned with oregano and basil, homemade or prepared
2 whole large eggs or 4 egg whites
2 tablespoons freshly squeezed lime juice or Meyer lemon juice
1/4 cup pure maple syrup
1 1/4 teaspoons sea salt or kosher salt
1/2 teaspoon cayenne

Special Equipment:

1 standard-size metal loaf pan (if using oven-proof glass adjust time as it may finish faster)

Penne with Meat-Laden Tomato–Morel Sauce

This meat sauce has a definite morel flavor! The recipe makes 16 cups of sauce—perfect for a meal or two and plenty to freeze! Use homemade or prepared pasta, preferably whole wheat or vegetable noodles. The sauce also serves admirably for a full-blown lasagna.

Yield: 16 cups

Ingredients for Sauce:

4 ounces dried morels, brushed, reconstituted, drained (liquid reserved and divided)

1 1/2 tablespoons olive oil

3 medium-large sweet yellow onions, peeled and chopped

3–4 cloves garlic, peeled and finely chopped

3 pounds grass-fed beef, ground (or ground meat of your choice), broken into small pieces

2 large (28 ounce) cans petite-diced tomatoes, including juice

2 (6 ounce) cans tomato paste

1/2 cup red wine (preferably Cabernet Sauvignon)

2 1/2 cups reserved morel liquid

3 tablespoons finely chopped fresh basil

1 tablespoon finely chopped fresh oregano

1–2 teaspoon crushed red pepper flakes (for mild spice, stick with 1 teaspoon)

1 cup low-sodium beef stock, homemade or prepared (plus additional if necessary)

Salt (depending on saltiness of stock)

Directions:

In a large nonstick sauté pan, insides coated with cooking spray, cook morels with 1/2 cup morel liquid over medium heat, for about 6 minutes; set aside. When cool enough to handle, process morels to a rough chop with a food processor, or chop with a knife; set aside. You should have 3 cups of chopped morels.

Place a very large round Dutch oven, saucepan (8 quart or larger), or stockpot over medium heat and add olive oil. When hot, add the chopped onions and garlic; cook 12 minutes or until nicely browned. Add the ground meat. Reduce heat to medium-low and continue to cook until the meat is no longer pink, 9–10 minutes, stirring frequently. If any unwanted grease collects, remove with a baster or spoon and discard.

Add diced tomatoes (including juice) and tomato paste; stir and cook for about 5 minutes. Add wine and 2 1/2 cups of reserved morel liquid; cook over medium-low heat for 15 minutes, or until it comes to a full boil.

Reduce heat to simmer, cook about 30 minutes, then add basil, oregano, and red pepper; cook 10 minutes. Add the cooked chopped morels and 1 cup of beef stock.

Continue to cook sauce 2 hours on simmer, stirring occasionally. Add more beef stock if necessary to desired consistency. Adjust seasoning—only add salt if necessary.

While the sauce is in last stages of simmering, cook the pasta according to package directions, preferably al dente. Drain pasta well prior to serving.

Serve the hot pasta with the sauce; 4–6 cups of sauce will easily coat a pound of pasta, but you can adjust according to desired proportions. Add some Parmigiano–Reggiano as a garnish, if desired. Serve pasta accompanied by a deep-green crisp side salad.

Ingredients for Pasta:

1 pound penne pasta or pasta of
your choice (preferably whole
wheat). *Note:* 1 pound of pasta
should easily feed 6 adults

Freshly grated Parmigiano-Reggiano
(optional garnish)

Note: Make sure to use at least 4
cups of water in reconstituting the
morels—you need quite a bit of
reserved liquid for this recipe.

Pork Tenderloin and Morel Wraps

These luscious wraps are loaded with goodies–including homemade hoisin (whose recipe is in Additional Tips). For a great presentation, leave the filled lettuce leaves open with ingredients showing and place them in old-fashioned banana split dishes, then let guests fold their own wraps. Serve with a side of stir-fried vegetables sprinkled with sesame seeds.

Yield: 6 large lettuce wraps (or make them smaller and serve as an appetizer)

Ingredients:

1 1/4 ounces dried morels, brushed, reconstituted, and drained (liquid reserved)

2 cups brown sticky rice cooked according to package directions

3/4–1 pound small pork tenderloin, trimmed of fat, rinsed, and patted dry

2 tablespoons hoisin sauce, homemade (see Additional Tips, p. 125) or prepared

Splash of Mirin (sweet Asian cooking wine), about 1/4 cup

30 Asian pea pods, trimmed and rinsed

4–6 scallions, green parts only (or an equal amount of chives), cut diagonally into 1/2 inch pieces

Red leaf lettuce or romaine leaves, trimmed, washed well, and dried (any lettuce will work—red leaf is particularly pliable)

Additional hoisin sauce to coat inside of lettuce leaves (optional)

Directions:

Preheat oven to 350°F. Place oven rack to middle position.

In a large nonstick sauté pan, add morels and about 1/4 cup of reserved mushroom liquid; cook over medium heat 6 minutes or until liquid is absorbed. Set aside; when cool enough to handle, cut the morels in half lengthwise.

Coat a small ovenproof pan generously with cooking spray and add pork tenderloin. Brush hoisin sauce on pork tenderloin (both sides) and bake for 35–40 minutes until well cooked (160–165°F). At the 30-minute mark, splash bottom of pan with Mirin (about 1/4 cup); stir—it will make a brown gravylike sauce. Remove from oven and let cool slightly. *Note:* As with all meats, the temperature will rise as the meat rests out of the oven. When cool enough to handle, place pork on a cutting board and cut into thin diagonal slices; either chill for later preparation or place back in the oven for just a few minutes to absorb the pan liquid. *Note:* If chilling, when ready to assemble, reheat oven and put pork back in the sauce to just take the chill off, 5–10 minutes.

In a small saucepan filled with about an inch of water, set in collapsible steamer; add pea pods, and steam for 6–8 minutes or until pods are bright green and crisp. Remove steamer with pea pods and place under cold running water to stop the cooking process. Set aside; when cool enough to handle, slice in thin strips lengthwise.

Lay lettuce leaves flat, spread interior lightly with hoisin sauce (optional). In the center of each leaf using equal amounts for each leaf, layer with sticky brown rice (1/3 cup), pea pod, scallions, slices of pork tenderloin, and morel halves. Fold over right and left sides of lettuce leaves to form a wrap and place on a serving platter; or serve open with ingredients layered in center and placed in individual banana split dishes.

Special Equipment: Collapsible steamer (to fit in saucepan)

Sometimes, you just want a piece of medium-rare red meat! Piedmontese beef or bison are great options when it comes to a flavorful rib eye. Serve sauced steaks with fluffy mashed potatoes and steamed fresh asparagus. The morels are definitely highlighted in this hearty entrée.

Rib-Eye Steaks with Red Zin–Morel Sauce

Directions:

In a large nonstick sauté pan, add reconstituted morels and 1/2 cup of reserved liquid; cook over medium-high heat for 6–8 minutes (adding more liquid if necessary during cooking process); stirring frequently. When morels have absorbed all liquid, remove from heat and cool slightly; place in a bowl. Cut the morels in half lengthwise (or if very small, keep them whole); set aside.

In a 12-inch nonstick sauté pan or heavy skillet, heat oil over medium-high heat until oil appears to shimmer; sauté the rib eyes (don't crowd pan; do in shifts as necessary), about 3 1/2 minutes each side for medium-rare (or cook to desired doneness—if cooking bison, keep it medium-rare). *Note:* Turn steaks only once.

Repeat with remaining steaks. Transfer to a platter and cover with aluminum foil to hold temperature.

There should not be much oil left; if more than a teaspoon or two, remove excess oil but not the brown pan bits. In the same pan, sauté garlic over medium heat until light brown, about 1 minute. Add wine and bring to a boil, stirring constantly and scraping the bottom of the pan until liquid is reduced by half, about 3 minutes. Add morel liquid, ponzu, and any juice collected from the steak platter; reboil until reduced slightly. Reduce the heat to medium low and whisk in the butter substitute and rosemary; add morels. Divide the wine sauce and morels equally and spoon over each steak.

Yield: 4 servings

Ingredients:

1 1/2–2 ounces dried morels, brushed, reconstituted, and drained (at least 1 cup liquid reserved, divided)

4 boneless rib-eye steaks (1/2-inch thick), preferably piedmontese beef or bison, rinsed in cool water and patted dry with paper toweling

2 tablespoons olive oil

6 garlic cloves, peeled and finely chopped

1 1/2 cups red zinfandel (*Note:* the better the wine, the better the sauce)

1/2 cup reserved morel liquid

2 1/2 teaspoons ponzu (or citrus-flavored soy sauce)

4 tablespoons butter substitute

4 teaspoons chopped fresh rosemary

Duck Breasts with Blackberry–Morel Sauce

These duck breasts with morel sauce are the perfect entrée for dinner guests. They look elegant and taste complex, flavorful, and rich. Serve with mashed potatoes and a deep-green chopped salad.

Yield 4–6

Ingredients:
Olive oil cooking spray/olive oil
1 ounce dried morels, brushed, reconstituted, and drained (liquid reserved)
1/2 cup sliced ramps (or leeks)—white part only, washed, trimmed, and sliced
2 tablespoons low-calorie butter substitute
2 tablespoons turbinado or natural cane sugar
1 cup white wine (preferably Riesling)
2 tablespoons seasoned rice vinegar
1 pound fresh blackberries, rinsed and well drained
1 1/2 cups low-sodium chicken stock
1/4 cup crème de cassis
2 tablespoons pure maple syrup
4–6 duck breast halves (6 ounces each) with skin on

Special Equipment:
Barbecue Grill

Directions for Preparing the Blackberry Sauce:
Coat the inside of a small sauté pan with cooking spray and place over medium heat. Add morels and sauté with about 1/4 cup reserved morel liquid. Cook for about 6 minutes. Set aside; when cool, slice all but 12 morels into rounds. Halve the remaining morels and set aside.

In the same sauté pan, cook the ramp slices for 4–5 minutes, until lightly brown in color; set aside.

Melt 2 tablespoons butter substitute in heavy saucepan over medium heat. Add 2 tablespoons sugar; stir until dissolved and mixture turns a deep golden color (about 6 minutes—keep in mind that turbinado sugar starts out brown in color). Add wine and rice vinegar (the sugar will recrystallize); bring to boil, about 2 1/2 minutes, stirring to dissolve sugar again. Add 2 cups of blackberries and chicken stock; boil for about 45 minutes until sauce thickens and is reduced to about 1 1/2 cups, stirring the mixture periodically. Set aside; when cool enough to handle, place blackberry mixture into a food processor and process until smooth; place back in heavy small saucepan. Add sautéed morels and sautéed ramps; add crème de cassis and maple syrup. Mix well and bring mixture back to boil. Set sauce aside while cooking duck breasts.

Directions for Grilling the Duck:
Coat grill grate with cooking spray or dampen a papertowel with olive oil and wipe grate.

Preheat grill to medium-high. Trim any excess fat from duck breasts.

Place duck breast filets skin side down on grill; sear until nicely browned and marked with grill marks (4–5 minutes). Turn down grill to medium and turn filets over to cook other side (about 3 minutes). Check duck breasts to make sure they are not cooking too fast. Cook an additional 3–4 minutes or until to desired doneness is reached.

Reheat sauce if necessary. Place some sauce in the center of each plate; add cooked duck breast to center of sauce and garnish with fresh, uncooked blackberries and some of the halved morels.

Place some additional morel halves on top of the duck and serve.

Arctic char is the perfect fish to accompany this earthy morel sauce. This entrée is quick and easy and can be made after a full day of work or served to company for a special dinner. Remember to use a good-quality white wine (or alcoholic cider) for the best results. The cream sauce can be done with fresh or dried-and-reconstituted morels. If fresh, the blondes are perfect! Then again, any morels are perfect.

Arctic Char Fillet with Morel Mushroom Cream Sauce

Directions for the Arctic Char:

Preheat oven to 350°F. Set oven rack to middle position.

In an ovenproof baking dish, add 1/2 tablespoon of the Garlic Essence and brush over the surface; place fillets on baking dish. Brush remaining 1 1/2 tablespoon of garlic–olive oil mixture on fish, then place in oven. Bake 25–30 minutes or until the fish is cooked and very lightly browned.

Directions for the Sauce:

While the fish is baking, coat a medium-sized nonstick sauté pan with cooking spray and cook morels for 6–8 minutes over medium heat. Place morels in a bowl; when cool enough to handle, halve the morels lengthwise; set aside momentarily.

In the same sauté pan resprayed with cooking spray, sauté the shallots until wilted, 2–3 minutes. Add the garlic and continue to cook for about 1 minute; set aside.

In a medium-sized saucepan, add the olive oil and heat over medium heat. Whisk in the flour and make into a bubbly paste, about 3 minutes. Slowly add the wine or cider, whisking constantly. Add coconut milk and keep whisking, to a light boil, until thickened, about 6 minutes. Pour the creamy contents of the saucepan into the shallots pan and deglaze, mixing with a spoon (preferably wooden), until smooth. Reduce heat to very low. Add morels and stir until thoroughly combined; add tarragon, salt, and white pepper and continue to cook on very low heat for 3 minutes or until the morels and tarragon have infused the sauce.

Remove the cooked Arctic char from the oven and serve with morel cream sauce. Serve with a steamed green vegetable and some wild rice, quinoa, or crispy baked potato slices.

Yield: 4 servings

Ingredients for the Arctic Char:

1 pound Arctic char fillet, rinsed in cool water and patted dry with paper toweling

2 tablespoons RMJ's Garlic Essence (see Additional Tips, p. 126)

Ingredients for the Morel Cream Sauce:

Olive oil cooking spray

3/4 pound fresh morels (preferably blondes, but any will do), brushed, lightly rinsed, and halved

2 tablespoons peeled, finely minced shallots

2 cloves garlic, peeled and finely minced

2 tablespoons olive oil

2 tablespoons all-purpose flour

1/2 cup white wine or alcoholic cider (preferably Woodchuck) *Note:* The cider may give a bit sweeter result

1 cup light coconut milk

1 tablespoon fresh tarragon, finely chopped

1/4 teaspoon salt

1/16 teaspoon white pepper

Morel and Black Bean Burgers

Finding a great vegetarian burger can be a task—these Morel and Black Bean Burgers will be a real hit for lunch or dinner. And special enough for guests, but make sure there are no nut allergies to contend with. Serve on very thin whole wheat sandwich buns, or, for those watching carbs, serve on a large lettuce leaf for a wrap. I don't serve these burgers with condiments, as I want the morels to stand out!

Yield: 4 vegetarian burgers

Ingredients:
Olive oil cooking spray/olive oil
3/4 ounce dried morels, brushed, reconstituted, and drained (liquid reserved)
1 small red onion, peeled and chopped
3 cloves fresh garlic, peeled and rough chopped
1/8 cup sliced jalapenos (from a jar)
1 (15 ounce) can black beans, rinsed and drained (or cook your own)
1/2 cup finely ground almonds or pecans
1/2 cup whole wheat panko (or plain whole wheat bread crumbs)
1 egg

Directions:
In a nonstick pan sprayed with cooking spray, sauté morels for about 4 minutes (adding 2–3 tablespoons of reserved morel liquid. Add the chopped onions to the morel pan and continue to cook and stir for 3 minutes, or until onions are lightly browned. Set aside to cool slightly.

In a food processor, add the morels, onion, garlic, and jalapenos; process on pulse, keeping ingredients distinguishable (or chop by hand). Remove ingredients to a large bowl.

In the same food processor bowl, add black beans and, again, process quickly on pulse. Remove beans and add to the bowl containing the morel mixture.

To the mixture, add the nuts, Panko, and egg; mix thoroughly.

Divide the black bean morel mixture into four equally sized balls and pat into burgers. The mixture will hold together like a meat patty.

Heat a large nonstick frying pan with a bit of olive oil (or spray) over medium-high heat. Gently fry burgers on each side until crispy, 3–4 minutes per side, making sure they are heated through. Once cooked, set on paper toweling if necessary to drain any unwanted oil. Place burgers in thin sandwich buns or wrap in a lettuce leaf and serve.

This delicate soufflé has been a favorite at Northern Michigan mushroom events since I developed the original recipe for Joe Breidenstein's Mushroom Weekends in Walloon Lake. This recipe started from the original and accommodates those of us watching our fat intake. It is still a perfect balance of eggs, cheese, and the prized morels! For a nice flavor and color addition, add some chopped chives. Serve with steamed asparagus and some crusty rolls.

Morel Soufflé à la Healthy

Directions:

Preheat oven to 375°F. Set oven rack to middle position.

Grease an ovenproof soufflé dish (using 3/4 tablespoon of butter substitute) and set aside.

In a large nonstick sauté pan, heat the remaining butter substitute until melted; add morels. Sauté mushrooms (5–6 minutes). Let cool; when morels are cool to the touch, slice into rounds and set aside.

In a blender or food processor, process the eggs, half-and-half, Parmigiano–Reggiano, mustard, salt, and pepper, until well blended and smooth.

Add the cheddar cheese and reprocess, just to mix. Add the cream cheese in small amounts until well blended. Remove cheese mixture to a bowl and stir in the morels, mixing thoroughly.

Place the soufflé ingredients into the greased soufflé dish and bake at 375°F for 70 minutes or until top is golden brown and springs back when gently tapped with your finger. Remove the soufflé from the oven and serve immediately.

Note: Check soufflé at 60 minutes for doneness; timing will vary depending on baking dish. If soufflé seems to brown too quickly, turn heat down slightly.

Yield: 6–8 servings

Ingredients:

2 ounces dried morels, brushed, reconstituted, drained (liquid reserved), or use fresh equivalent
2 tablespoons butter substitute, divided
6 large eggs
1/2 cup fat-free half-and-half
1/4 cup freshly grated Parmigiano–Reggiano cheese
1/2 teaspoon Dijon-type or any deep-flavored mustard
1/2 teaspoon sea salt
1/4 teaspoon white pepper
4 ounces low-fat (reduced-fat cheddar cheese, shredded
11 ounces light cream cheese, softened

Special Equipment:

Soufflé dish (6–8 cups), or any ovenproof baking dish with some height.
Blender or food processor

Roulades of Chicken Stuffed with Morels, Leeks, and Almonds

Stuffed chicken breasts loaded with goodies—you won't have to be searching for stuffing in these roulades as they are generously filled with morels, leeks, and almonds. Make sure before planning to serve that your guests have no nut allergies. Serve with a nice portion of wine-infused pan juice, some mashed potatoes, and deep-green veggies.

Yield: 4 servings

Ingredients:

2 plump whole chicken breasts, split (4), removed from bone and skinned (or preboned and skinned)

8 ounces fresh morels (preferably blonde), lightly brushed and wiped clean, halved lengthwise, and sliced into rounds

1 1/2 tablespoons olive oil

3 1/2 cups sliced leeks (white and light green parts only), well rinsed

1/8–1/4 cup plus 2 tablespoons white wine (preferably Chardonnay), divided

1 teaspoon red pepper flakes

1 cup sliced raw almonds

Olive oil cooking spray

1/4–1/2 teaspoon sea salt

Directions:

Preheat oven to 350°F. Set oven rack to middle position.

On a flat surface, gently pound split chicken breasts (1 at a time), with metal meat tenderizer, between 2 sheets of plastic wrap, until they are 1/4 inch thick or slightly thinner. Take care not to make holes in the flesh. Repeat process until all 4 are thinly pounded; discard plastic wrap and set aside.

In a large nonstick sauté pan, heat the olive oil over medium heat; add leeks and sauté for about 9 minutes, Add fresh morel slices and continue to sauté for about 3 minutes; splash with 2 tablespoons of white wine. Turn heat down to medium-low and add pepper flakes; continue to cook for about 9 more minutes. Stir in almond slices, mix well, and remove from heat.

On a clean surface, lay chicken breasts (1 at a time) smooth side down; add 1 cup of the morel/almond mixture to the center of the cutlet and fold like a package, enclosing mixture on all sides (pulling meat carefully over the stuffing). Flip over, place seam-side down. Repeat with remaining ingredients, making 4 stuffed chicken-breast roulades.

Generously spray low-sided baking dish with cooking spray. Place completed roulades seam-side down in baking dish; spray each roulade with cooking spray and sprinkle with sea salt. *Note:* Wooden picks can be used to secure closure if necessary.

Bake roulades 45 minutes or until pan juice is browned. In the last five minutes of cooking, splash with remaining white wine and mix with the pan juice.

Remove roulades from pan and cut in half on the diagonal. For serving, place both halves on individual plates exposing the stuffing. Spoon browned pan juice over each roulade and serve.

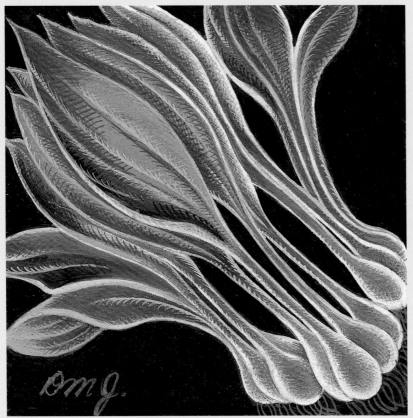

Courtesy Earthy Delights

Special Equipment:
Metal meat tenderizer (hammer-
   type)
Plastic wrap
Low-sided baking dish to
   accommodate the 4 stuffed
   roulades

Sea Scallops, Morels, and Ramps in a Light Cream Sauce

Simple and elegant, these scallops and morels are perfect served over a bed of wild rice. Serve as a dinner entrée, appetizer, or luncheon entrée. If serving for dinner, add a crisp green salad with fruity vinaigrette and some steamed asparagus wrapped with strips of pimento.

Yield: 4 servings

Ingredients:

2 cups cooked wild rice, prepared according to package directions
16 large sea scallops, rinsed well and patted dry
1/4 cup whole wheat flour (for dusting)
3 tablespoons olive oil, divided
6 ounces fresh morels, lightly rinsed, drained, and halved
1/4 cup chopped ramps (white and light green parts only), or shallots, peeled and chopped
10 large sprigs flat-leaf parsley, roughly chopped
1 cup fat-free half-and-half
1 1/4 teaspoons sea salt

Note: Make sure to have some lead time for the rice.

Directions:

Prepare wild rice and set aside.

Lightly dust the scallops in flour; set aside.

In a large nonstick sauté pan, heat 2 tablespoons of olive oil over medium heat; add morels and cook 3–4 minutes, stirring frequently. Add chopped ramps or shallots and cook an additional 3 minutes. Add fresh parsley; lightly toss and move all ingredients to the outsides of the pan, leaving the center open for the scallops.

To the center of the pan, add the remaining tablespoon of olive oil; heat on medium-high, then add the dusted scallops. Cook about 2 minutes on each side. Quickly pour the half-and-half over scallops and cover the pan. At 3 minutes, lift lid and turn scallops over; cook an additional 2 minutes (make sure not to overcook scallops—total cooking time should be about 7 minutes, depending on size of scallops). Turn off heat; add salt and gently mix all ingredients.

To serve, place 1/2 cup of wild rice on each entrée plate; divide the scallops equally and top with morels and sauce.

Love those Asian flavors and aromatics? Here is a treasured combination of ingredients to produce that fix! Combining red curry with the highlight of shrimp and morels makes for a triumph in this Thai-inspired entrée.

Shrimp and Morel Mushroom Red Curry

Yield: 4 generous servings

Ingredients:

32 fresh morels, brushed, lightly rinsed if necessary, and halved lengthwise

24 large to extra-large raw shrimp, peeled, deveined, and rinsed in cool water

2 1/2 tablespoons light olive oil, divided

1/2 cup sweet yellow onion, peeled and finely chopped

1 full stalk lemongrass, trimmed and peeled slightly, fresh light portion cut into slices

2–5 Thai red peppers. *Note:* To cut down heat, you can remove the seeds

3 cloves garlic, peeled

1-inch piece galangal, peeled and sliced (available at Asian groceries, usually in the freezer section)

3 tablespoons canned tomato paste

2–2 1/2 teaspoons agave nectar

2 teaspoons ground cumin

1 teaspoon freshly ground coriander seeds

1/4 teaspoon ground white pepper

3 tablespoons Thai fish sauce (lowest sodium possible)

1 tablespoon tiny dried shrimp (from the Asian grocery)

1 1/2 cans light coconut milk (21 ounces total)

1 lime, juiced, or juice of 1 Meyer lemon

Fresh cilantro or Thai basil, trimmed, washed, and rough chopped

Directions:

In a large nonstick sauté pan over medium heat; add 1 tablespoon olive oil. When hot, add the fresh morel halves and sauté for 6–8 minutes or until well cooked; set aside.

Drain the shrimp well and refrigerate in an open glass container until ready for use.

In a food processor or blender, process onion, lemongrass, chiles, garlic, galangal, tomato paste, agave nectar, cumin, coriander, white pepper, fish sauce, and dried shrimp. *Note:* This mixture is your recipe for a fragrant Thai-style red curry paste.

In a clean nonstick sauté pan over medium heat, add remaining tablespoon of olive oil; fry the curry paste until aromatic. Slowly add the light coconut milk in a steady stream, stirring to incorporate it into the curry paste, creating a smooth-textured sauce. When thoroughly mixed, add the lime juice and cook for 6–10 minutes to thicken. Once thickened, add the reserved shrimp and morels; cook until shrimp appear opaque, 3–6 minutes. Do not overcook shrimp! Garnish finished dish with fresh cilantro or Thai basil.

Serve Shrimp and Morel Red Curry with some hot naan and steamed deep-green vegetables.

Garlic Shrimp and Morel Stir-Fry with Sesame Seed Crêpes

If making this recipe in spring or early summer, feel free to use fresh morels instead of reconstituted, and in place of the pea pods, use crisp fiddlehead ferns! You can use sesame seeds of your choice—white, black, and wasabi are available separately at Asian groceries; this combination adds color and a very mild wasabi taste. The crêpes can be used with anything savory; once you start making them, you will find lots of ways to incorporate them in your cooking. Serve crêpes with steamed broccoli or asparagus and a side of mandarin oranges.

Yield: 10 crêpes, about 4 servings

Ingredients for Crêpes (10):
1/2 cup whole wheat flour
1/2 cup all-purpose flour
1/4 teaspoon salt
2 eggs (or 4 egg whites)
1 cup fat-free half-and-half
1/4 cup water
2 teaspoons olive oil
4 tablespoons sesame seeds
   (preferably a mix of white, black, and wasabi)
Olive oil cooking spray

Special Equipment:
sifter
8-inch nonstick sauté pan (for making crêpes)
Whisk
Ladle or spoon that will accommodate 3 tablespoons
Parchment paper (to separate crêpes)

Directions for Crêpes:
Sift both flours and salt into a medium-sized bowl. Make a well in the center of the flour and set in eggs; slowly add half-and-half and water, whisking as you add. When bubbles form on the edge of the batter, add in olive oil; mix thoroughly. Add sesame seeds and mix.

Coat a small nonstick sauté pan with cooking spray and place over medium heat; when hot, quickly add 3 tablespoons of batter, tilting the pan quickly with your wrist so that the batter spreads all over the bottom and a bit up around the edge. Cook for 1 minute 15 seconds to 1 1/2 minutes, until top of crêpe appears dry and edges are lightly browned; with the tip of a dull knife, lift to see color of the crêpe's surface; if brown enough to your liking, gently flip the crêpe over with your fingertips, holding it at the edge (be careful of the heat!). Let second side of the crêpe cook until light brown, again for up to 1 1/2 minutes. Slide the crêpe off the pan to a plate and cover with a piece of parchment paper. Repeat the process with the remainder of the batter—you should have 10–11 crêpes. Make sure to spray pan between crêpes.

Note: The first one is usually the test crêpe—taste it to make sure the batter is perfect. Also, the crêpes can be made a day ahead and reheated. It gets easier, once you get the hang of it!

Directions for Stir-Fry:

In a large nonstick sauté pan or wok, add reconstituted morels and 1/2 cup of reserved liquid; cook over medium-high heat for about 6 minutes, stirring frequently and adding more liquid if necessary during cooking process. When morels have absorbed all liquid, remove from heat and cool slightly; place in a bowl or container. Cut the morels in half lengthwise (or if very small, keep them whole); set aside.

In the same pan, add 3 tablespoons of butter substitute and melt over medium-high heat; add garlic slices and continue to cook for about 1 1/2 minutes. Add raw shrimp and cook until color changes, about 2 1/2 minutes per side; remove shrimp from pan to a clean dish or bowl (leaving garlic in the pan); set aside. Turn the heat down to medium, and in the same pan, add the pea pods; cook 3 minutes or until bright green. Add scallion and stir; continue cooking for about 2 minutes.

Add reserved cooked morel halves and sauté 1 1/2–2 minutes. Add cooked shrimp back into the pan and splash with the Mirin or white wine. Sprinkle with fresh parsley and salt; stir to mix well and remove from heat.

Serve the stir-fry with the sesame seed crêpes and have guests make their own wraps. Want to add a more of an Asian influence? Have some hoisin sauce on hand (see Additional Tips, p. 125), just in case guests would like to accent their crêpes.

Ingredients for Stir-Fry:

2 1/2 ounces dried morels, brushed, reconstituted, and drained (liquid reserved)

1 1/4 pound large shrimp (20–24), peeled and deveined

3 tablespoons butter substitute

4–5 cloves garlic, thinly sliced (about 1/4 cup)

32 fresh Asian pea pods (3 1/2–4 ounces), trimmed and rinsed

3/4 cup diagonally sliced scallions (green parts only)—cut in 1-inch pieces

1/4 cup Mirin (sweet Asian cooking wine) or any white wine of your choice

2 tablespoons chopped fresh parsley

1/4 teaspoon sea salt

Lake Trout Stuffed with Asparagus, Leeks, and Morels

Surprise your dinner guests with hidden morels (fresh or reconstituted) in this stuffed trout ... serve with a side of wild rice, basmati rice, or coconut-flavored brown rice and a crisp fruited dark-green salad. Make some Garlic Essence (see Additional Tips, p. 126) for this recipe and to keep on hand for others—a great staple!

Yield: 4 servings

Ingredients:

2 tablespoons RMJ's Garlic Essence (see Additional Tips, p. 126), divided
1 cup sliced leeks (white and light green parts only), rounds well rinsed and drained
1 cup fresh morels, brushed or wiped clean, quickly rinsed if necessary, and drained
20-ounce lake trout fillet, rinsed in cool water and patted dry
14 spears of raw fresh asparagus (top 4-inch portion), trimmed and rinsed.
Olive oil cooking spray

Special Equipment:

1 large metal skewer (at least 6 inches in length)

Directions:

Preheat oven to 350°F. Set oven rack to middle position.

In a medium-large nonstick sauté pan add 1 tablespoon of Garlic Essence and heat to medium-hot; add leek rounds and sauté 3–4 minutes or until tender (don't brown). Remove from heat; place cooked leeks in a small bowl and set aside to cool.

In the same sauté pan, add remaining Garlic Essence and sauté morels over medium heat, 6–8 minutes. Remove from heat; when cool enough to handle, slice whole morels crosswise into rounds; set aside.

On a clean flat surface, lay trout fillet out (skin-side down). Place cooked leeks in center of trout; top crosswise with spears of asparagus (tips will show once fished is closed). Top asparagus with cooked morel rounds.

Bring up one side of the trout, then the other, overlapping to close (skin will now be on the topside); secure with a metal skewer piercing the flesh of the fish to completely close. Make sure morels are hidden (they are to be a surprise). Coat with cooking spray a low, relatively small baking dish that will comfortably accommodate the fish; place stuffed fish in center of the baking dish and coat skin of fish with cooking spray. Bake for 35–40 minutes or until fish skin begins to lightly brown and flesh still feels a bit firm to the touch (baking time will vary depending on the thickness of the fish). Remove skewer from fish for serving. Cut into sections making sure each guest receives some of each of the stuffing goodies.

Big Water.
The Ojibwa (North American) Native American means of
fishing at night (Legend painting)

Thin-Crust Grilled Pizza with Tomato, Spinach, and Morels

This delicious thin-crust crisp pizza makes for a great entrée or appetizer. Add or subtract your favorite ingredients, but this is a great combination!

Yield: 2 large thin-crust or 4 small thin-crust pizzas

Ingredients for Dough:
1 cup warm water (110 to 115°F)
1 1/2 teaspoons turbinado sugar (regular sugar will also work)
1 envelope fast-rise yeast or 2 1/2 teaspoons bread-machine yeast
2 cups all-purpose flour
1 cup whole wheat flour
1 teaspoon kosher salt
2 tablespoons olive oil, plus additional oil for greasing bowl
Yellow cornmeal

Special Equipment:
Barbecue grill
Pastry brush

Directions for Dough:
In a glass measuring cup, combine the warm water, sugar, and yeast; mix well. Let mixture stand until foamy, about 5 minutes.

In the bowl of a food processor, add flour and salt; process just to combine.

Add yeast-mixture and oil; process until dough comes together and forms a ball, about 1 minute.
Remove dough from food processor and knead gently on a clean, flat surface for about 30 seconds. Dough should feel light, smooth, and elastic.

Lightly oil a large glass bowl; place dough ball inside and, with a sharp knife, cut a big X into the dough. Cover tightly with plastic wrap. Let stand in warm, draft-free area until dough doubles in size, 45 minutes to 1 hour.

Remove plastic wrap and punch down dough while in bowl; remove dough and lightly knead.

Divide the dough into two or four equal-sized balls; cover with plastic wrap and place in the refrigerator until ready to use (you can use this time to prepare your topping).

Note: If making this dough without the aid of a food processor, mix ingredients in a glass bowl with a fork, then follow directions in recipe.

Putting It All Together:

In a large nonstick sauté pan coated with cooking spray, sauté morels for about 6 minutes; set aside. When cool enough to handle, cut into halves or fourths (depending on size of morels). Set aside.

Generously coat a clean grill rack with cooking spray or dampen a paper towel with olive oil and wipe grate. Prepare grill to medium heat.

In a food processor, combine the olive oil, garlic, and parsley for base of pizza; set aside.

Sprinkle a clean, flat surface with yellow corn meal. Coat hands lightly with flour to handle dough; remove dough balls, one at a time, from the refrigerator. Pat dough down into a disk using the heel of your hand; roll out into a thin circle or desired shape, keeping it about 1/4-inch thick (it puffs up a bit while cooking).

Transfer the rolled out dough top-side down (not the cornmeal side) onto the prepared grill; lid the grill. Cook dough for 4 minutes, or until the top crust is lightly browned. Remove from grill and brush with oil–garlic mixture; top with tomato, morels, red onion rings, spinach, and cheese. Return the topped pizza to the grill; cover the grill and cook until the cheese melts or ingredients are warmed through, 5–6 minutes.

Remove pizza from grill, let rest a couple of minutes, and cut into slices or portions.

Grill as many pizzas as you have room for on the grill. And, if your grill does not have a lid, cover pizzas loosely with aluminum foil.

Ingredients for Pizza:

Olive oil cooking spray

2 ounces dried morels, brushed and reconstituted (liquid reserved)

1/4 cup olive oil

3–4 cloves of garlic, peeled

1/4 cup flat-leaf parsley (no stems)

1 pkg. "on the vine" medium-small red ripe tomatoes, sliced

1 large red onion, peeled, thinly sliced, and rings separated

1/2 cup cooked spinach (or more if desired), well drained

8 ounces chèvre cheese, chilled

Turkey, Morel, and Trompette Sausages with Chipotle Remoulade

Crazy for encased meats? Here is an unusual sausage loaded with white-meat turkey, morels, black trompettes, and fresh herbs and topped with a spicy remoulade. Don't do spicy? Leave it off and add your own favorite condiments. Be creative and come up with your own toppings!

Yield: 9 large sausages that will fit on a hot dog bun, or 18–24 small, breakfast-sized links

Ingredients for Sausages:

2 1/4 ounces dried morels, brushed, reconstituted, and drained (liquid reserved, divided)

3/4 ounce dried black trompette mushrooms, reconstituted and drained (liquid reserved) (*Note:* Reconstitute the mushrooms together)

2 pounds ground turkey (white meat only)

3 small fresh red hot peppers, seeded, deveined, and chopped

4 tablespoons fresh sage, finely chopped

2 tablespoons fresh parsley, chopped

2 teaspoons fresh lemon thyme leaves (or use regular fresh thyme and 1/2 teaspoon lemon juice)

4 tablespoons fresh chopped chives

2–3 cloves garlic, peeled and minced

1 1/2 teaspoons ground cumin

2 1/2 teaspoons kosher salt

1/4 cup plus 1 tablespoon reserved mushroom liquid

2 egg whites (use large eggs)

Directions for Sausages:

In a large nonstick sauté pan, cook morels and trompettes over medium heat for about 9 minutes with 1/4 cup (or more) reserved morel liquid. The morel liquid will be absorbed by the end of cooking time. Let mushrooms cool to the touch and add to the bowl of a food processor; chop on pulse and set aside.

In a large, nonreactive bowl, add the ground turkey, peppers, sage, parsley, thyme, chives, garlic, cumin, salt, 1/4 cup plus 1 tablespoon mushroom liquid, and egg whites; mix thoroughly. Add chopped mushrooms and incorporate into the mixture.

Take about 1 tablespoon of the turkey/mushroom mixture and place in a nonstick sauté pan and cook thoroughly. Taste the sausage and make any seasoning adjustments necessary prior to stuffing the casings.

Utilizing a sausage stuffer, KitchenAid mixer with attachment, or equipment of your choice, stuff the turkey/mushroom mixture into the casing and separate into links. If making full-size, you should yield 9. Set aside when completed.

Coat grill grate with cooking spray or dampen a paper towel with olive oil and wipe grate. Preheat grill to medium-high. Place sausages on grill and cover grill. Cook for 10–12 minutes and turn over; continue to grill for an additional 10–12 minutes or until sausages have grill marks and appear well cooked.

While the sausages are cooking, prepare the remoulade. In a food processor, add chipotle peppers, adobo sauce, lime juice, chèvre cheese, half-and-half, and salt. Process until all ingredients are smooth and well mixed. Add more half-and-half if you prefer a thinner sauce.

When sausages are cooked, place in individual buns, top with 1–2 tablespoons of remoulade, and sprinkle with additional chèvre cheese crumbles (if desired). Serve with a side of cole slaw and handful of baked vegetable chips.

Courtesy Earthy Delights

3 feet hog casing (options for
    smaller casings are lamb and
    sheep)
Olive oil cooking spray
hot dog buns
additional chèvre cheese for topping
    (optional)

**Ingredients for Chipotle Remoulade
(makes 1 cup):**

1 can (7.5 ounces) chipotle peppers
    in adobo sauce (you will use
    2 peppers, chopped, and 2
    teaspoons of the sauce; save
    remainder for another recipe)
1 1/2 tablespoons fresh-squeezed
    lime juice (juice of 1 lime)
3/4 cup chèvre cheese plus extra as
    a garnish, or creamy tofu
1/4 cup fat-free half-and-half (or
    more depending on desired
    consistency)
1/4 teaspoon salt

Special Equipment:
Sausage stuffer
Grill

Stuffed Grape Leaves with Morels and Brown Rice

A great entrée, appetizer, or side dish, these grape leaves are Middle Eastern-flavored, healthy, and nutritious. Pick up some lamb neck bones from the grocery or your butcher to enhance the flavor. And make sure to prepare the lentils before you start your recipe. Cooked stuffed grape leaves can be frozen for later use. This is a big project—perfect for weekends!

Yield: Big batch (about 70)

Ingredients:
6 ounces dried morels, brushed, reconstituted, and drained (liquid reserved)
Olive oil cooking spray
1 1/2 tablespoons olive oil
1 very large sweet yellow onion, peeled and finely diced (3 cups)
2 large cloves garlic, minced
6 cups finely diced green cabbage
2 cups peeled, shredded carrot
3 cups cooked black (beluga) lentils
2 1/2 cups raw brown rice, rinsed very well
1 can (28 ounces) diced seasoned tomatoes, well drained (save juice for another recipe)
1 tablespoon lemon juice
2 tablespoons chopped fresh mint
1 tablespoon plus 1 teaspoon Baharat Spice (see Additional Tips, p. 127)
2 teaspoons kosher salt (or more to taste)
1/4 teaspoon ground white pepper

Directions:
In a large nonstick pan sprayed with cooking spray, sauté the morels for 6–7 minutes; remove to a large bowl and set aside. When cool enough to handle, chop and set aside.

In the same nonstick pan, heat the oil over medium-high heat. Add the onions and sauté until transparent (about 6 minutes); add garlic and cook an additional 2 minutes. Add cabbage and cook for 7 minutes longer. Add carrots and cook 3 more minutes. Remove vegetables from heat.

Add the cooked vegetables to the morels, along with the lentils and washed brown rice. To that mixture, add the tomatoes, lemon juice, mint, Baharat Spice, salt, and white pepper; mix well. Adjust seasonings if necessary.

Leave the rinsed grape leaves in a large bowl with cool water and work one leaf at a time. Drain each leaf and place it with the stem and veins facing up on a flat surface. Remove any bit of stem at the base. Place one tablespoon of the stuffing mixture (more depending on the size of the leaf) onto the lower center of the leaf. Pull the leaf bottom over the mixture, and roll gently, folding in the sides as you go. Make sure the rolls are tight. Repeat with remaining leaves and stuffing mixture until all the stuffing is gone.

Coat with cooking spray the bottom and sides of a very large Dutch oven (or several, depending on the size), stockpot, or large kettle with a lid. Line bottom of pot with flat lamb neck bones and top with spare flat grape leaves. Arrange the stuffed leaves over the bones and loose leaves—place horizontally or vertically in a single layer in the bottom of your pan. Repeat the process, each layer in a direction different from that of the previous layer. Pour the lemon juice, water, and oil mixture over the layered stuffed leaves. Cover the pot and bring to a rapid boil. Once boiling, reduce the heat to simmer and cook for 1 1/2 hours, or until the stuffed leaves are cooked and the water is almost evaporated. At the hour mark, check to make sure there is still liquid in the pot; you don't want it to boil out and cook dry. Check one grape leaf to make sure the rice is thoroughly cooked. (*Note:* Keep in mind that brown rice takes longer to cook than white rice.) When cooked, turn off heat and let sit for about 20 minutes, leaving the lid in place.

Note: If you want to keep it vegetarian, replace bones with ribs of celery or thick slices of peeled onions.

Serve Stuffed Grape Leaves warm, or chill and serve cold. Serve with Laban if desired.

1 16-ounce jar grape leaves, drained and rinsed well (have an additional small jar on hand in case some leaves are unusable), or use fresh

3/4 cup lemon juice

1/2 cup water

1 tablespoon olive oil

Lamb neck bones, trimmed of as much fat as possible and cut into 1 to 1 1/2-inch slices (to cover bottom of pot)

Heavy yogurt (Laban; see Additional Tips, p. 125) to use as a sauce if desired (use plain or add a little chopped garlic and chives)

Wild Game Loin with Morel–Red-Wine Sauce

I chose antelope loin for this recipe, but you should feel free to use any wild game or even beef tenderloin. The antelope is easily purchased over the Internet; or check out specialty meat shops. Remember when cooking game, don't overcook! This lean meat needs to be prepared medium-rare or rare. With no visible fat, you just can't cook it too long. Check your temps!

Yield: 4 servings

Ingredients for Sauce:

1 1/2 tablespoons olive oil
1 1/2 cups fresh morels, lightly brushed and wiped clean or lightly rinsed if necessary (preferably small whole morels or larger morels, halved lengthwise)
2 cloves garlic, peeled and minced
3/4 cup red wine (preferably Cabernet Sauvignon)
1 cup low-sodium veal or beef stock (homemade or prepared)
1 tablespoon finely chopped fresh flat-leaf parsley
1 teaspoon finely chopped fresh thyme
1 tablespoon tomato paste
1/4 teaspoon freshly ground black pepper
1 tablespoon butter substitute (optional)

Directions for Sauce:

In a medium-sized nonstick sauté pan, add olive oil and warm over medium heat; add morels and sauté for 5–6 minutes. Add the garlic and continue to sauté another minute.

Turn heat to medium-high and deglaze the pan with red wine; reduce by half (about 6 minutes).

Add veal or beef stock and continue to cook until all pan liquid is reduced by half (about 12 minutes). While sauce is simmering, add parsley, thyme, tomato paste and pepper; stir to mix in paste thoroughly. *Note:* Keep a close watch on liquid—morels will soak a lot of it up!

Check seasonings and adjust as necessary. Remove pan from heat; set aside while meat is being prepared.

Directions for Meat:

Coat grill grate well with olive oil cooking spray or dampen a paper towel with olive oil and wipe grate. Preheat grill to high; once hot, reduce heat to medium.

Place loin on grill grate; cover grill and cook for about 8 minutes *Note:* Cooking time will vary depending on meat chosen, thickness, and desired doneness.

Turn meat over and spray top of meat with olive oil if it appears dry; cover and cook for an additional 8 minutes or to desired doneness.

Prairie Fire.
The Mandan Sioux (North Dakota/Missouri River) Native American with a
pronghorn antelope draped across the back of the horse (Legend painting)

When cooked (for medium rare game to about 120°F), remove meat to a serving plate and let rest 5–7 minutes (meat will rise in temperature, about 10°, once removed from heat and has time to rest). While meat is resting, gently rewarm the morel sauce; whisk in butter substitute if desired.

Slice loin into equal portions (8 or 12 slices depending on size of meat), or plate individual tenderloins, and serve with Morel Red-Wine Reduction Sauce.

Ingredients for Meat:
Olive oil cooking spray/olive oil
1 and 1/2 pounds antelope loin
    or any game meat or beef
    tenderloin.

Note: If serving individual tenderloins, serve 1 per person; if doing a loin, cook whole and slice for serving.

SIDE DISHES

David McCall Johnston

Ale-Flavored Brown Rice with Morels, Shallots, and Sage

This is a flavorful side dish and needs to accompany a strong entrée—perfect for beef, game meat, pork, or lamb. Serve family style or place in an oiled mold and serve as a shape of your choice. The mold really makes for a dramatic presentation!

Directions:

In a large nonstick sauté pan, add morels and about 1/2 cup of reserved mushroom liquid; cook over medium heat 8–9 minutes or until liquid is absorbed. Set aside; when cool enough to handle, cut the morels in half lengthwise (if small, leave them whole). Place in a large bowl.

In the same sauté pan add olive oil and sauté shallots over medium heat for about 6 minutes. Remove the shallots and add to the bowl with the morels; mix well.

To the bowl, add cooked shallots, warm brown rice, sage, and peas; mix thoroughly. Season with salt and mix well. Adjust seasoning if necessary.

Coat the molds of choice with cooking spray and place each mold on a salad plate or dish; to the mold, add desired amount of rice and morel mixture (1/2–1 cup); press firmly. Gently lift mold from the dish; serve alongside entrée. Or, serve family style in a serving bowl.

Yield: 4 cups—will serve 4–8 depending on size of mold used

Ingredients:

1–1 1/4 ounces dried morels, brushed, reconstituted, and drained (liquid reserved)

2 cups brown rice, washed well, and, using dark ale as the liquid, cooked in a rice cooker or according to package directions (about 3 cups cooked rice)

1 bottle (12 ounces) ale (preferably British), to cook the rice in (if you need more liquid, add a bit of water)

6 shallots, peeled and minced (about 3/4 cup)

1 1/2 tablespoons olive oil

1 tablespoon chopped fresh sage

1 cup cooked peas (or Wasabi peas)

1/4 teaspoon salt

Olive oil cooking spray

Note: You can make molds out of brand new, washed PVC piping cut to the height you choose, or use purchased molds with open ends—diamond-shaped molds are lovely.

Morel, Scallion, and Hoisin Pork Farro

Farro—one the "super grains"—is high in protein and looks akin to brown rice, although plumper and nonclinging, with great texture and great fiber.

Serve this Asian-inspired side dish in 1/2-cup ramekins for a measured and attractive presentation. Sprinkle with sesame seeds or extra scallion if desired. This is a great accompaniment to any meal with a meat, fish, or poultry entrée.

Yield: 8 (1/2 cup) servings

Ingredients:

Olive oil cooking spray

1/2–3/4 pound pork tenderloin, trimmed of fat, rinsed, and patted dry

2 tablespoons hoisin sauce, homemade (see Additional Tips, p. 125) or prepared

1 ounce of dried morels, gently brushed and reconstituted (liquid reserved)

2 cups or raw semipearled farro, cooked in a rice cooker with low-sodium chicken stock, or in a pot according to package directions

1/2 cup chopped scallions (white and green parts)

1 tablespoon Mirin (sweet Asian cooking wine)

1/4 teaspoon ponzu (or citrus-flavored soy) sauce

Sesame seeds for garnish (optional)

Special Equipment: 8 (1/2 cup) ovenproof ramekins

Directions for Asian-Inspired Farro:

Preheat oven to 350°F. Place oven rack to middle position. Coat 8 ramekins with cooking spray. Set aside.

Coat a small ovenproof pan with cooking spray and add pork tenderloin. Brush hoisin sauce on pork tenderloin and bake for 35–40 minutes until well cooked (160–165°).

Remove pork from oven and let cool. Once cool, cut into small cubes. *Note:* As with all meats, the temperature will rise as the meat rests out of the oven.

Coat the insides of a large sauté pan with cooking spray; cook morels over medium heat with a splash of reserved morel liquid; sauté for about 6 minutes. Add scallions and cook an additional 2 1/2 minutes; splash with Mirin. Let cool slightly.

Place morels and onion mixture in a food processor and process on pulse to rough chop, or roughly chop with a knife.

In a large bowl, add cooked farro, cooked pork cubes, morel–onion mixture, and ponzu; mix thoroughly. Divide the mixture evenly into 8 ramekins. Top with additional scallion or sesame seeds if desired. Serve or reheat slightly, if necessary.

Three of these little potato puffs are about equal in size to an ice cream scoop (about 1/2-cup)—two or three small ones on a plate make a nice presentation. Or, bake it in a casserole dish to serve family style. These light puffs go with just about anything—lamb, game meat, chicken, veal, beef, fish, and seafood.

Morel and Ricotta Potato Puffs

Directions:

Preheat oven to 350°F. Set oven rack to middle position. Place Silpat® or parchment on baking sheet (or coat with cooking spray); set aside

In a medium-sized nonstick sauté pan, add reconstituted morels and 1/4 cup of reserved liquid; cook over medium heat for 6–8 minutes (adding more liquid if necessary during cooking process); stir frequently. When morels have absorbed all liquid, remove from heat and cool slightly; finely chop morels in a food processor or with a knife, and set aside.

In a medium-large round Dutch oven or saucepan filled with cool water, add potatoes (making sure potatoes are all about the same size; cut them into pieces if necessary) and boil over medium-high heat until fork tender (about 30 minutes). Drain potatoes.

In the bowl of an electric mixer fitted with the whisk attachment, add potatoes and mix slightly. Add Garlic Essence, parsley, half-and-half, ricotta, egg, and salt. Mix until light and fluffy, about 2 minutes. Stir in the morels; mix thoroughly. Adjust seasoning if necessary. Potato mixture should not be too wet, but mashed potato-like.

With the cookie scoop, scoop out a ball of potato mixture and set on covered baking sheet. Repeat the process with the remaining potato mixture. Place in oven and bake for 30 minutes or until warm and lightly crisp on top. *Note:* These puffs do not spread. With a spatula, remove to a serving platter or to individual dinner plates.

Yield: 30 small potato puffs (8–12 servings)

Ingredients:

1–1 1/4 ounce dried morels, brushed, reconstituted, and drained (liquid reserved)

3 pounds of small red potatoes, scrubbed and rinsed, skins left intact

2 tablespoons RMJ's Garlic Essence (see Additional Tips, p. 126)

2 tablespoons fresh chopped flat-leaf parsley

1/4 cup fat-free half-and-half

2/3 cup ricotta cheese (homemade or prepared)

1 large egg, lightly beaten

1/2–3/4 teaspoons sea salt (to taste, depending on saltiness of the ricotta)

Special Equipment:

Mixer with whisk attachment (or potato masher)

Silpat® silicone sheet or parchment paper

Baking sheet

Cookie scoop/48 mm scoop (optional, if making multiple puffs)

Fillo Bundles with Morels, Onion, and Napa Cabbage

These crisp Fillo (Phyllo) Bundles can be served as a side dish or appetizer. Asian inspired, they can accompany almost any chicken, fish, or meat entrée. They make a dramatic presentation that can be served in or out of ramekins. Prepared fillo dough is available in the refrigerated sections of grocery stores.

Yield: 6–12 servings (1 or 2 per guest)

Ingredients:
Olive oil cooking spray
1 1/2 tablespoons olive oil
1/2 cup peeled, chopped red onion
8 ounces fresh morels, cleaned and halved
1/4 cup cognac
8 cups roughly chopped napa cabbage, top part only, rinsed well
2 tablespoons hoisin sauce, homemade (see Additional Tips, p. 125) or prepared
1 tablespoon whole wheat flour
12 sheets fillo dough (9 × 14)

Special Equipment:
12 ramekins (1/2 cup capacity) or 12-cup muffin tin

Directions:

In medium-sized nonstick sauté pan coated with cooking spray, cook onion over medium heat (3–4 minutes). Remove to large bowl; let cool.

In the same sauté pan, add olive oil and heat over medium heat; add morels halves and cook about 4 minutes. Add cognac and cook an additional 4 minutes. *Note:* Between rinsing morels and cognac, you will have liquid left in pan; leave it there. Remove morels to bowl with onions.

In the same sauté pan, with liquid remaining, add cabbage and cook for about 4 minutes, stirring until cooked down to about 2 1/2 cups. Remove to bowl with onions and morels. Add hoisin and mix well. Sprinkle mixture with flour and mix thoroughly. Set aside.

Preheat oven to 350°F. Set oven rack to middle position.

Place 1 sheet of fillo dough on baking sheet and spray with cooking spray; repeat with next two layers. Lay down fourth sheet (don't spray). Cut the 4 layers of stacked dough into quarters. Coat 1 ramekin with cooking spray and lay in 1 quarter of stacked dough. Add 1/4 cup of filling to center of fillo (will fit in bottom of ramekin); gently pull the loose 4 corners of fillo together and twist to close. Coat the tops of the fillo bundles with cooking spray. Repeat entire process with remaining 3 sections, creating 4 bundles. Begin the process again with four more sheets of fillo and filling (making another 4 bundles). Repeat the entire process until you have 12 bundles.

Place the 12 bundle-filled ramekins on a baking sheet and bake for 20–25 minutes or until golden brown and crisp (check timing–it could vary depending on type of fillo used). *Note:* If using a muffin tin, there is no need for a baking sheet, but remember to spray each cup with spray before adding bundles.

Serve in or out of ramekins (if using muffin tins, remove and serve).

Morel and Potato Kugel

This pudding-like dish is crusty on the outside and soft on the inside—the perfect bite! The addition of morels is a showstopper . . . guests will beg for more. Offer them as a side dish to any entreé with which you would serve potatoes.

Yield: 8–10 servings

Ingredients:
1 3/4 ounces dried morels, brushed, reconstituted (liquid reserved)
1 cup fresh flat-leaf parsley leaves (loosely packed)
1 tablespoon fresh lemon thyme leaves (or use regular fresh thyme and 1/2 teaspoon lemon juice)
12 red potatoes (about 2 1/2 inches each), skins intact, scrubbed well
1 large red onion, peeled
1 large carrots, peeled and rinsed
3 eggs (or 6 egg whites), lightly beaten
1 teaspoon baking powder
1 1/2 teaspoons kosher salt
3 tablespoons olive oil

Special Equipment:
8 × 10 inch rectangular pan (if using a larger pan, you will probably have to reduce the baking time—keep watch!)
Silicone or other heat-resistant pastry brush

Directions:
Preheat oven to 375°F. Set oven rack to the middle position.

In a large nonstick sauté pan, add morels and about 1/4 cup of reserved liquid; cook over medium heat for 6 minutes or until liquid is absorbed. Set aside. When cool, place in a food processor. Add parsley leaves and lemon thyme. Process morels and herbs on pulse to rough chop (or rough chop with a knife). Set aside.

Using a hand grater, grate potatoes, onion, and carrot; place in a large bowl.

To the mixture add eggs, baking powder, and salt; mix. Add morels and herbs; mix thoroughly.

Add 3 tablespoons of olive oil to pan and place in oven for 5–7 minutes to heat pan and oil. With pastry brush, coat the entire pan well with the hot oil. Reduce heat on oven to 350°F. Place all of the potato ingredients into the pan and place in oven.

Bake for 60–70 minutes or until kugel is browned and crisp on top.

This summertime favorite is perfect any time of year; having fresh basil growing in the garden makes it easy. Add veal, stir-fried chicken, or seafood and call this side dish an entrée!

Morel Pesto Pasta Salad

Directions:

In a large nonstick sauté pan with 1 1/2 tablespoons of olive oil, sauté the morels over medium heat for 8–9 minutes; set aside. When cool cut morels in half lengthwise; set aside.

In the bowl of a food processor, process fresh basil leaves, olive oil, chicken stock, pine nuts, garlic, parsley, and salt. When the mixture is well blended and smooth, pour into a bowl; stir in cheese.

In a very large bowl, toss the Romaine lettuce, pasta, and morels with enough pesto just to coat.

Serve Morel Pesto Pasta Salad with a small bowl of any remaining pesto for guests to add, if desired. This salad is best at room temperature.

Yield: 6–8 side-dish servings

Salad Ingredients:

1 1/2 tablespoons olive oil

3 cups fresh morels, brushed and lightly rinsed (if using dried, follow process for reconstituting)

3 1/2 cups cooked (al dente) bow tie or tricolor farfalle pasta (5 ounces dry)—follow package directions and drain well

1 small–medium head romaine lettuce, washed, trimmed, and dried

Ingredients for Pesto:

2 cups packed fresh trimmed basil leaves (about 1 3/4 ounces, without stems)

1/2 cup olive oil

1/4 cup low-salt chicken stock (homemade or prepared)

1/2 cup pine nuts

2–3 garlic cloves, peeled

2 tablespoons fresh chopped flat-leaf parsley

1/2 teaspoon sea salt

1 cup freshly grated Parmesano–Reggiano cheese

Polenta with Sautéed Morels, Red Onion, and Garlic

Talk about comfort food—here is the perfect combination! Corn and morels make a great duo for this popular side dish. You can use your shaped polenta as a bed for an entrée, or stack it with ingredients between layers and serve as a first course.

Yield: 9 × 13 rectangle of polenta–big batch

Ingredients:

Olive oil cooking spray

2 ounces dried morels, brushed, reconstituted, and drained (liquid reserved)

1 1/2 tablespoons olive oil (plus extra for grilling or sautéing if desired)

1 red onion, peeled and finely chopped (about 3/4 cup)

1 tablespoon finely minced garlic

1 quart low-sodium chicken stock (homemade or prepared)

1 cup coarse ground cornmeal (available at some markets and specialty and health food stores)

2 tablespoons low-fat butter substitute

1/2 teaspoon sea salt (if desired, depending on saltiness of stock)

1/8–1/4 teaspoon ground white pepper or cayenne

1/2 cup Parmigiano–Reggiano cheese, freshly grated

Directions:

Preheat oven to 350°F. Set the oven rack to the middle position.

Line a 9 × 13 × 2-inch cake pan with parchment paper cut to fit the bottom of the pan.

In a medium-sized sauté pan well coated with cooking spray, sauté morels for about 4 minutes, add about 1/4 cup of the retained mushroom liquid, and continue to sauté for another 4–5 minutes. Remove from heat. When cool enough to handle, rough chop the morels; set aside.

In a medium-sized round Dutch oven or medium-large ovenproof saucepan with a lid, heat the olive oil over medium heat; add the onion and sauté until it becomes translucent, about 3 minutes. Reduce heat to low; add minced garlic and continue to sauté for about 1 minute.

In the same pan, add chicken stock; turn up the heat to medium-high and bring the stock to a boil, about 8 minutes. Gradually add in the cornmeal; whisking continually. Turn off heat; cover pan and let sit undisturbed for about 5 minutes. Place the covered polenta in the oven and bake for about 30 minutes, stirring every 10 minutes to prevent the formation of lumps. Remove pan from the oven and add butter substitute, salt (if necessary), and pepper. Gradually add cheese and morels; mix thoroughly. Adjust seasoning if necessary.

Place the morel-infused polenta into the parchment-lined pan; let cool slightly. Lightly cover the pan with plastic wrap. Place the polenta in the refrigerator to cool completely.

Once set, turn out the chilled polenta onto a clean cutting board and cut into whatever shapes desired—circles, squares, triangles, or simple cookie-cutter shapes. Brush each side with olive oil and lightly grill in a nonstick skillet well coated with cooking spray, over medium heat, or place on heated grill. *Note:* Make sure your grilling surface is well oiled, or polenta will stick!

Serve the morel-infused polenta as a side dish to accompany poultry, fish, or meat. And save the scraps from the cutouts to serve later pan fried with eggs!

Special Equipment:
Wire whisk
9 × 13 × 2 inch baking pan
Parchment paper
Cookie cutter of your choice
    (optional)

Pumpkin and Morel Risotto

Nothing says fall like pumpkin and other winter squash. This risotto makes a special side dish in the fall months or anytime of the year. If you can't get fresh pumpkin or squash, use canned. It won't be quite the same because you won't have any diced bits, but the flavor will be there! The combination of squash, morels, and pepitas are about as earthy as you can get.

Yield: 6–8 servings

Ingredients:
- 1 1/4 ounces morels, brushed, reconstituted, and drained (liquid reserved)
- 1 medium-sized pie pumpkin or winter squash, halved, seeded, and rinsed (if using canned you will need 1 cup total), divided
- 1/4 teaspoon freshly grated nutmeg
- 1/2 teaspoon ground ginger
- 1/4 teaspoon ground cloves
- 3/4 teaspoon finely minced fresh sage
- 3 cups low-sodium chicken stock (homemade or prepared)
- 2 tablespoons olive oil
- 3/4 cup thinly sliced leek (white and light green parts only), carefully rinsed and drained
- 1 1/2 cups arborio rice
- 1/2 cup white wine
- 1/2 cup freshly grated Parmesano–Reggiano cheese
- 1/2 cup fat-free half-and-half
- Pepitas (hulled pumpkin seeds) for garnish (optional)

Directions:

Preheat the oven to 400°F. Set oven rack to middle position.

In a medium-sized sauté pan over medium heat, sauté morels in 1/4 cup reserved liquid for 8–9 minutes. Remove from heat; when cool enough to handle, slice morels into rounds; set aside.

Place both halves of the pumpkin or squash with the inside facing down in a baking pan with 1/2–1 inch of water. Place in oven and bake just until tender but not mushy (check with a fork), 30–75 minutes (depending on type squash). Remove from oven and place cut-side up on a platter to cool enough for handling. Scoop out the soft flesh of one of the halves with a spoon and place in a food processor. Add nutmeg, ginger, cloves, and sage; process until smooth; set aside. Peel the second squash half (the skin will peel easily) and cut into small dice; set aside.

In a medium-sized saucepan over low heat, bring the chicken stock to a simmer. In a second pan (medium–large), add olive oil and heat over medium heat. Add the leek slices and cook until lightly brown, about 4 minutes. Add the rice and stir for about 2 minutes. Add white wine and simmer for another 2 minutes until the liquid is absorbed, stirring constantly.

Set a kitchen timer for 20 minutes. Add half a cup of hot stock to the risotto and stir constantly until it is absorbed. Add another half cup of stock and repeat this process, adding half cups (reserving 1/2 cup stock) until the 20-minute timer goes off.

Add the spiced pumpkin purée and final half cup of stock; stir briskly. When the risotto has become thick and creamy, add the diced squash and grated cheese; restir to combine. Adjust seasonings if necessary. Stir in half-and-half and cooked morel rounds; mix thoroughly and top with pepitas. Serve alongside your entrée.

Note: My favorite squash is a crossbred of pumpkin, Rouge Vif d'Étampes, and sweet dumpling squash—feel free to use whatever type of squash you prefer (though sweeter is better).

This unusual stuffing is a great accompaniment to any poultry, game meat, or pork. Subtly sweet and loaded with morels, it is a delicious combination! Make some RMJ's Garlic Essence (see Additional Tips, p. 126) for this recipe and keep some extra on hand for other recipes.

Raisin Bread and Morel Stuffing

Directions:

Preheat oven to 350°F. Set oven rack to middle position.

Coat a large baking sheet with cooking spray. Place thick raisin bread cubes on sheet and bake for 30 minutes until crisp. Set aside to cool.

Coat a large sauté pan or Dutch oven with cooking spray. Over medium heat, sauté the leek rounds for 2–3 minutes or until wilted. Add to the pan 1 tablespoon of the Garlic Essence and cook the celery for 5–6 minutes, stirring occasionally. Add parsley, rosemary, and sage and continue to cook 1 more minute. Remove vegetable–herb mixture to a large bowl.

In the same sauté pan or Dutch oven, add another tablespoon of Garlic Essence and cook the morel rounds for 5–6 minutes. To the pan, add in the leeks, celery, herbs, and raisin bread cubes. Over medium-low heat, stir the mixture and add in 1/2 cup of chicken stock and 1/2 cup reserved morel liquid. If mixture appears too dry, add more liquid.

Coat an ovenproof serving casserole or baking pan with cooking spray and pour in the entire mixture. Bake at 350°F until heated through and crisp on the top as you like. Serve warm as an accompaniment to your main dish

Yield: 8 (1/2 cup) servings

Ingredients:

Olive oil cooking spray

2 tablespoons of RMJ's Garlic Essence (see Additional Tips, p. 126)

4 cups raisin bread cut into cubes (best to use a bread that has not been sliced)

1 1/2 ounces dried morels, brushed, reconstituted, and sliced into rounds (liquid reserved)

1 1/2 cups leeks, white and light green parts only, sliced into rounds, well rinsed, and drained

3 ribs of celery with leaves, chopped (about 1 cup)

1/4 cup fresh chopped fresh flat-leaf parsley

1 1/2 teaspoons chopped fresh rosemary

1 1/2 teaspoons chopped fresh sage

1/2 cup low-sodium chicken stock, homemade or prepared

1/2 cup retained morel liquid

Morel, Quinoa, and Potato Pancakes

Some preliminary preparation is required for these delicious pancakes, but they are definitely worth the effort. You can make mini-pancakes for an appetizer or use two pancakes as a bed for a cooked fish, seafood, or chicken entrée.

Yield: 8 side-dish–sized pancakes

Ingredients:

1 1/2 cups cooked quinoa (cook as you would rice in a rice cooker, or follow package instructions)

1 1/4 ounces of dried morels, brushed and reconstituted (about 2 1/2 cups when reconstituted), liquid reserved

Olive oil cooking spray

3 cups raw, hand-shredded russet potato

1 cup scallions, washed and sliced into rounds (green part only)

3/4 cups all-purpose flour

1 1/2 teaspoon salt

1/4–1/2 teaspoon ground cayenne

3 large eggs (or 6 egg whites)

Olive oil

Special Equipment:

1/2 cup measuring cup with a flat bottom

Directions:

Prepare quinoa as directed in ingredients list.

In a medium-large nonstick sauté pan coated with cooking spray, cook morels, about 6 minutes, stirring frequently. Remove from heat; when cool, slice into rounds and set aside.

In a large bowl, mix together shredded potato, quinoa, morel rounds, scallions, flour, salt. and cayenne. Add eggs and remix so all ingredients are well blended.

Heat a little olive oil in a large nonstick pan; when hot, add 1/2 cup of morel–potato mixture. Using the flat bottom of a measuring cup, press down on the pancake to flatten it slightly. Repeat with three more pancakes. Let brown on one side and flip over to brown the other side. Remove browned pancakes to a piece of paper toweling to drain; repeat the process again with the remaining ingredients (another 4 pancakes). If necessary, place the first batch in an ovenproof dish and put in a warm oven to keep warm while remaining pancakes are prepared.

Serve when all 8 pancakes are completed.

These stuffed potatoes are a great accompaniment to almost any entrée. Keep the potatoes small to medium . . . none of us need a crater-sized potato! Don't let your stuffing get too wet; you want them to be fluffy yet stiff enough to stay in place when rebaked. Salt isn't necessary due to the cheese—if adding any, do it sparingly.

Baked Potatoes Stuffed with Morels and Cheese

Directions:

Preheat oven to 375°F. Place oven rack to the middle position.

In a medium-sized nonstick sauté pan coated with cooking spray, sauté morels with a little reserved liquid (2 tablespoons). Cook morels for about 8 minutes; set aside; when cool enough, slice the morels into rounds and set aside.

Pierce each potato in several areas with the tines of a fork. Place potatoes on the oven rack and bake until tender, 45 minutes–1 hour. Check doneness at the 45-minute mark. If potatoes are soft when you squeeze them, they are done.

Using an oven mitt or clean dishtowel to hold potatoes, cut the top of each potato lengthwise. Cut a small amount of potato from the top and discard only the circle of cut-off skin, not potato. Scoop cooked potato flesh from each potato with a spoon and place in the bowl of an electric mixer, leaving the potato skin intact. Add flesh from the tops. Add butter substitute, half-and-half, and both cheeses. Using the whip attachment, turn mixer on and whip. Season with black pepper and check seasonings; add morels and remix gently.

With a spoon, mound mashed potatoes into potato skins (mounding high). Sprinkle tops lightly with paprika. Place double-stuffed potatoes in a baking dish coated with cooking spray. When ready to serve, preheat oven to 350°F. Rebake potatoes until heated through, 25–30 minutes. Serve warm as a side dish. *Note:* These potatoes can be made a day ahead, refrigerated, and rewarmed.

Yield: 4 double stuffed potatoes

Ingredients:

1 ounce dried morels, brushed, reconstituted, and drained (liquid reserved)
Olive oil cooking spray
4 small–medium baking potatoes
3 tablespoons butter substitute
1/2 cup fat-free half-and-half
2 tablespoons shredded Parmesano–Reggiano cheese
2 ounces reduced-fat cheddar or colby cheese, shredded
1/8 teaspoon freshly ground black pepper
Salt (optional—remember, the cheese contains salt!)
Paprika (for garnish)

Mélange of Garden Vegetables and Morels

Garden fresh vegetables are always a great side dish. This versatile dish offers not only an interesting combination, but the morels add a unique quality and texture. Ratatouillesque . . . the flavors are bold! Serve at room temperature. Caution for those allergic to fish.

Yield: 4 servings

Ingredients:

1 1/2 ounces dried morels, brushed, reconstituted, and drained (1 cup liquid reserved and divided)

1/4 cup olive oil

3–4 anchovy fillets, finely minced

4 large shallots, peeled and finely chopped (about 1 cup)

4 garlic cloves, peeled and finely chopped

16 okra, rinsed, trimmed, and cut into 1/2-inch slices (about 2 cups)

1/2 pound haricots verts (thin green beans), trimmed, rinsed, and halved (about 3 cups)

5 roma tomatoes, diced (about 2 1/2 cups)

1 dried or canned chipotle chile

Directions:

In a large nonstick sauté pan, add morels and about 1/2 cup of reserved mushroom liquid; cook over medium heat 8–9 minutes or until liquid is absorbed. Set aside; when cool enough to handle, cut the morels in half, lengthwise (if small, leave them whole); set aside.

In a medium-large saucepan over medium heat, add 1/4 cup olive oil. Add the anchovies; stir well and cook about 1 minute. Add shallots and cook for about 3 minutes; add garlic and cook 1 more minute. Add the okra and cook about 3 minutes; add haricots and cook an additional 2 minutes, stirring occasionally. Add diced fresh tomatoes and chile and cook on low for 10 minutes. Add all herbs, morels, and 3/4 cup reserved morel liquid; turn heat to low and continue to cook slowly for 15 minutes. Stir in finishing oil and balsamic vinegar; cool to room temperature. Adjust seasoning, if necessary, and serve.

Courtesy Earthy Delights

1/4 cup chopped fresh flat-leaf parsley

1/2 cup chopped fresh basil leaves

5 fresh lemon thyme leaves (or use regular fresh thyme and 1/2 teaspoon lemon juice)

1 tablespoon extra virgin olive oil (finishing oil)

3 tablespoons balsamic vinegar (good quality)

Yorkshire Pudding with Morel and Ale Gravy

Living in England for a while many years ago, I got hooked on Yorkshire Pudding. I not only ate a lot of puddings, I learned to make them "the British Way." With my interest in cutting down fat, I've come up with this new recipe! The old British trick was to use equal measurements for the milk, eggs, and flour, which I still do. Serve with Morel and Ale Gravy—it makes for a fabulous side dish! I do own a Yorkshire Pudding Pan (all tall cups connected), but this can be done in a traditional muffin tin. Mine come out really eggy and beautifully high!

Yield: 6–8, depending on size of Yorkshire pudding pan or muffin tin

Ingredients for Yorkshire Pudding:
4 large, fresh eggs, about 3/4 cup when measured
1/4 cup fat-free half-and-half
1/2 cup light coconut milk
1/8 teaspoon sea salt
3/4 cup all-purpose flour
2 tablespoons olive oil

Directions for Yorkshire Pudding:

Heat the oven to 450°F. Set oven rack to middle position.

In the bowl of an electric mixer, add eggs, half-and-half, coconut milk, and sea salt. With the whisk attachment, whisk on medium speed for 1 to 1 1/2 minutes, until all ingredients are well mixed. Let stand for 10 minutes.

Turn the machine back on and slowly sift the flour into the egg mixture using a small mesh sieve. Your batter should be lump free. Let the batter rest for at least 45 minutes.

Add 1/2 teaspoon of olive oil to each cup of a Yorkshire pudding pan or muffin tin. Place the oiled tin in the oven until it is almost smoking, about 7 minutes. When the pan is ready, add 2 tablespoons of cold water to batter and rewhisk. Fill to 3/4 full each cup of the pan or tin with the batter; quickly return to the hot oven.

Bake the Yorkshire Puddings until they puff up and turn golden brown, approximately 20–25 minutes. Serve warm with Morel and Ale Gravy.

Directions for Morel and Ale Gravy:

Heat a medium-sized sauté pan with 1 1/2 tablespoons of oil over medium heat and add fresh morels. Sauté for 6–8 minutes until they are soft and glistening. Add 2 tablespoons of browned chopped ramps or shallots; mix and sauté until thoroughly heated.

Add 1 cup of ale and cook about 3 minutes or until the mixture comes to a boil. Add 3/4 cup of the beef stock and bring back to boil.

To the remaining beef stock, add 1 tablespoon of cornstarch and whisk to mix; turn heat down to low and slowly stir in the cornstarch mixture. Continue to stir while the gravy cooks; stir until the gravy boil; keep stirring until it has body (not overly thick but gravy-like), about 6 minutes.

Serve warm Morel and Ale Gravy with the warm Yorkshire Puddings.

Ingredients for Morel and Ale Gravy:

1 1/2 tablespoons olive oil

6 ounces fresh morels, brushed or lightly rinsed, and drained (or the reconstituted equivalent).

2 tablespoons sautéed and browned chopped ramps or shallots

1 cup ale (preferably British ale)

1 cup beef stock (homemade or prepared), divided

1 tablespoon cornstarch

Special Equipment:

Small mesh sieve

Whisk

Sticky Brown Rice Packets with Morels, Ramps, and Chives

Try this unique Dim Sum favorite and pair it with your favorite meat or poultry entrée. Your meal does not need to be totally Asian influenced—mix and match ethnicities! Presentation is dramatic with the lotus leaves. Tie them with kitchen twine for a real package!

Yield: Serves 6 (one packet per person)

Ingredients:

Olive oil cooking spray

3/4–1 lb pork loin marinated in hoisin sauce (see Additional Tips, p. 125) with a little water and baked at 350°F for 45–55 minutes or until 170–180°F (or 2 cups of leftover cooked pork roast)

4 cloves garlic, peeled and minced

1 2-inch piece of ginger root, peeled and sliced

3 cups raw glutinous sweet brown rice

2 ounces dried morels, brushed, reconstituted, and drained (liquid reserved)

1/4 cup dried shrimp, rehydrated and squeezed dry

2/3 cup chopped scallions, white and green parts separated

1/2 cup Mirin (sweet Asian cooking wine)

1 tablespoon oyster sauce

Kosher salt (if necessary)

3 lotus leaves, soaked in warm water for 1/2 hour

Additional scallions or chives for garnish (optional)

Directions:

Cook pork loin or use leftover pork roast; diced small and set aside.

Make the sweet brown rice in a rice steamer as you would regular rice, or cook in a pot according to package directions. You need 4 cups of cooked rice. Transfer to a large bowl.

While rice is cooking, cook morels in a nonstick sauté pan over medium-high heat with some of the reserved liquid, for about 4 minutes. Set aside. When cool enough to handle, rough chop the morels.

Heat wok or large sauté pan over medium-high heat. Add oil and swirl to coat. Sauté garlic and ginger until lightly golden; add mushrooms and shrimp and stir-fry briefly (2–3 minutes).

Reduce heat to medium and add scallion whites and stir. Deglaze with mirin and reduce liquid completely (3–4 minutes). Remove to the bowl of a food processor and rough chop (or rough chop with a knife). Place the chopped ingredients into a bowl and add scallion greens and oyster sauce; stir. Pour mixture on top of reserved sticky rice (in large bowl). Mix well and check seasoning. Chill in refrigerator until cool enough to handle.

When sticky rice is chilled, cut lotus leaves in half and place about 1 cup sticky-rice stuffing in center. Fold lotus leaf around stuffing and wrap like a package. In wok or pot large enough to hold steamers, add water to just below bottom of steamer. Place packages in prepared bamboo steamers (or expandable steamer in a pot), seam-side down, cover, and steam over medium heat for 15–20 minutes, until heated through. Supply additional scallions for garnish.

Special Equipment: Stackable bamboo steamers or expandable steamer that fits in a pot with a lid

Out of season for fiddlehead ferns and ramps? No problem! Substitute with asparagus and scallions. These toast cups make a crispy and interesting presentation for a vegetable side dish—one per person.

Toast Cups Filled with a Mélange of Morels, Fiddleheads, Ramps, and Dried Cherries

Directions for Toast Cups:

Preheat oven to 350°F. Set oven rack to middle position.

Generously coat each cup of muffin tin with cooking spray. Using a rolling pin, roll flat 12 slices of bread, one at a time.

Place the open end of a jar or template on flattened bread; with a small sharp knife, follow the edge of the jar and cut out a 3 1/2-inch circle. On a flat surface, cut a slit in the circle from the center down (6:30 position on a clock).

Take bread disk and fit into muffin cup; overlap to fit perfectly. Bake for 10–12 minutes until lightly browned and crisp; remove from oven and set aside.

Note: Use remaining bread scraps with the center cut out for the breakfast treat "eggs in the basket." Cook scraps in an oiled skillet or nonstick sauté pan with eggs fried in the cutout center—flip over and cook the other side.

Directions for Filling:

In a medium-large nonstick sauté pan, add olive oil and heat over medium heat; add ramps and sauté for about 2 minutes. Add morels and sauté for about 2 minutes; add 1/2 cup reserved liquid and continue to cook for 6 minutes (liquid should be absorbed). Add fiddleheads and pea pods; cook about 1 1/2 minutes, stirring frequently.

Remove from heat and add salt, Mirin, and lemon juice; mix thoroughly. Add chopped cherries to mixture. Adjust seasonings if necessary.

Divide morel mixture evenly into prepared toast cups (sprinkle with sesame seeds if desired) and serve as a side dish to accompany any protein entrée.

Yield: 12 filled toast cups

Ingredients for Toast Cups:
Olive oil cooking spray
12 slices of whole wheat bread

Ingredients for Filling:
1 1/2 tablespoons olive oil
1/2 ounce dried morels, brushed, reconstituted, drained (liquid reserved), and rough chopped
1/2 cup ramps, trimmed and sliced (white and light purple part only)
1/3 cup fiddleheads, trimmed and rough chopped
1/2 cup rough chopped Asian pea pods
1/4 teaspoon kosher salt
1 1/2–2 tablespoons Mirin (sweet Asian cooking wine)
3/4–1 tablespoon freshly squeezed lemon juice (preferably Meyer lemon)
1/4 cup chopped dried cherries
Sesame seeds for garnish (optional)

Special Equipment:
Muffin tin (12-muffin capacity)
Rolling pin
3 1/2 inch round cookie cutter, jar lid, or circle template

Back from Shrooming

ADDITIONAL
◆TIPS◆

Heavy Yogurt (Greek Yogurt or Laban)

Homemade is best! In case you don't have time, though, there are also commercial products on the market for this purpose—check with kitchen shops or the Internet.

Yield: Will depend on how much liquid is in the yogurt and how long you drain it.

Ingredients:
One large container plain yogurt

Directions:
Place a container of plain yogurt in a fine mesh sieve, cloth-lined jelly strainer, or a sieve lined with cheesecloth. Set it in a bowl to catch the drippings. Allow the yogurt to drain, refrigerated, for 8–24 hours or to desired thickness. Keep refrigerated.

Hoisin Sauce

Hoisin sauce is available commercially, but for a real treat it is easy to make your own. Don't hesitate to adapt this recipe to your own taste.

Yield: 3/4 cup

Ingredients:
4 tablespoons ponzu (or light sodium-reduced soy sauce with a splash of citrus)
2 tablespoons peanut butter or black bean sauce
3 tablespoons tomato paste
2 tablespoons raw honey
2 teaspoons molasses
1–2 teaspoons agave nectar (or honey)
2 teaspoons seasoned rice vinegar
1/4–1/2 teaspoon Chinese five-spice powder
1/2 teaspoon chili sauce with garlic

Directions:
In a small bowl, whisk together all of the ingredients. Adjust seasonings to taste.

RMJ's Garlic Essence

Keep this on hand—so useful for many dishes and great on a slice of crusty bread!

Yield: about 1/2 cup

Ingredients: 1 bulb garlic, cloves peeled and trimmed
1/2 cup olive oil (good quality)

Directions:
Place garlic cloves in a small food processor or finely chop with a sharp knife. Remove garlic and place in a small glass bowl; add olive oil and mix thoroughly.

The Perfect Slather

Nothing like a crusty piece of bread slathered with roasted garlic and topped with some butter-substitute sautéed morels!

Directions:
Oven roast a garlic bulb coated in olive oil or olive oil cooking spray in a small low ovenproof pan at 400°F for 30 minutes or until cloves are soft. Squeeze out garlic to use as a spread on bread/biscuits or for a garlic ingredient in recipes.

Vinegar Dipping Sauce

Yield: 2/3 cup

Ingredients:
4 tablespoons ponzu (or light sodium-reduced soy sauce with a splash of citrus)
4 tablespoons brown rice vinegar
4 tablespoons Mirin (sweet Asian cooking wine)
2 tablespoons finely chopped scallion
4 teaspoons freshly grated ginger

Directions:
In a glass measuring cup or bowl, mix together the ponzu, vinegar, Mirin, scallion, and ginger. Place glass container in microwave oven for about 30 seconds or heat mixture in a pan over medium heat, just to a boil. Let cool down slightly and use as a dipping sauce—especially for steamed dumplings.

Garam Masala Spice Mix

Ingredients:
3 tablespoons coriander seeds
1 tablespoon cumin seeds
4 large cardamom pods
3/4 tablespoon whole black peppercorns
1 1/2 teaspoons black cumin seeds
2 teaspoons ground ginger
2 1-inch cinnamon sticks
3/4 teaspoon whole cloves
1–2 bay leaves

Special Equipment:
Designated "new" coffee or spice grinder specifically for spices

Directions:
In a nonstick sauté pan over medium heat, gently cook the coriander seeds, cumin seeds, black peppercorns, cumin seeds, whole cinnamon, whole cloves, and bay leaves, until they are fragrant and turn a few shades darker (stirring occasionally). Add the cardamom pods right before you remove from heat—don't over cook them. *Note:* do not cook the ground ginger.

Let spices cool to the touch. Once cool, remove the cardamom seeds from their pods and add to the roasted spices; place in the designated coffee or spice grinder and grind. Empty ingredients into a small bowl and add the ground ginger; mix thoroughly.

Store any unused Garam Masala Spice Mix in an airtight container in a cool dark place.

Baharat Spice Mix

Ingredients:
2 tablespoons paprika
2 tablespoons ground cumin
1 tablespoon ground coriander
1 tablespoon ground cloves
1/2 teaspoons white pepper
1 teaspoon nutmeg
1 teaspoon ground cinnamon
1/2 teaspoon ground cardamom
1/4 teaspoon sea salt (optional)

Directions:
Mix all spices together.

Store any unused Baharat Spice Mix in an airtight container in a cool dark place.

Homemade Spinach Pasta

Though a food processor and pasta machine make pasta making quick and easy, you can make this recipe without machines. Place the mixed dry ingredients on a flat surface and make a well in the center for the (already mixed) wet ingredients; combine thoroughly, then roll out with a rolling pin and place on the rack; follow instructions from there.

Yield: 26 (4–5 inch pieces of flat pasta noodles)

Ingredients:
3/4 whole wheat flour, plus extra for dusting flat surface
3/4 cup all-purpose flour, plus extra for process
2 egg whites
1 tablespoon olive oil
1 tablespoon Mirin (sweet Asian coooking wine)
3/4 cup chopped frozen spinach, thawed and well drained
   (for sun-dried tomato pasta, replace the spinach with
   3/4 cup crushed sun-dried tomatoes)

Special Equipment:
Food processor
Crank-handled pasta machine with accompanying vice grip
Lightly damp kitchen towel
Broom handle and 2 chairs and dry kitchen towels, or a
   commercial pasta-drying rack

Directions:
Set up the broom handle between 2 chairs and cover it with clean kitchen towels, or set out a pasta-drying rack.

In a food processor, add flours, egg whites, olive oil, Mirin, and spinach; process on pulse until dough comes together and forms a ball on top of the blade.

Sprinkle additional whole wheat flour on a clean, flat surface and remove dough ball from machine; knead the dough until it forms a ball that is smooth and elastic (only adding more flour if necessary).

Place pasta machine on a clean, flat surface and clamp with the accompanying vice to hold it in place. Dial the machine to #1 or the widest opening.

Remove a small, orange-sized piece of dough, flatten it, and put it through the machine, cranking it to the other side and forming a flattened piece. If the dough seems sticky, sprinkle it with additional all-purpose flour and redo. Make sure to put a lightly damp towel over the dough ball while you are working the individual balls of dough into noodles.

Change the dial on the pasta machine to #2 and repeat the process, move it to #3 and then to #4. At this point, you should have a nice even, flat piece of spinach pasta; lay the noodle over the covered broom handle to dry slightly. Repeat the process with the remaining dough. When completed, cut each noodle into a 4–5 inch piece, making sure longer noodles will fit in your lasagna pan.

When ready to cook your pasta, heat a large pot of water over medium-high heat; add a bit of olive oil. When it comes to a boil, put in your noodles and cook 8–9 minutes or until they are al dente (cooked but firm—"tender to the tooth"). Drain the noodles in a colander and use in your favorite recipe.

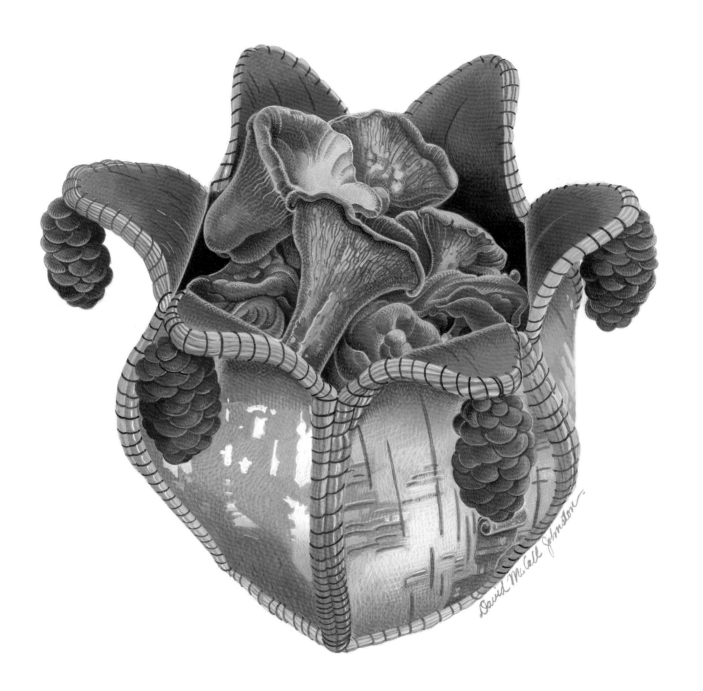

David McCall Johnstone

Tortillas

There are many options for tortillas—packaged, homemade, or prepared Masa dough—the choice is yours. The same is true for choosing a tortilla press; there are many types of construction. I use a hard plastic press, which is inexpensive, easy to clean, and always reliable. Making tortillas is definitely one of those things you need to practice—the more you make, the easier and quicker it becomes.

Ingrediants:
If I'm pushed for time and can't make my own dough, I use a packaged prepared dough called Masa Natural (Amarilla Para Tortillas)—it has no fat and is low in sodium.

Directions:
In using a tortilla press, I have found my own little tips that make it much easier: Try using 2 plastic quart-sized freezer bags to line your tortilla press. Coat each bag with olive oil cooking spray on one side, lay down one bag (spray side up), add your dough ball in center of press, lay down the second coated bag—face down, and bring down the top and push down the handle. Open the press and gently remove the top bag layer. Lift the bottom bag with the flattened dough ball (now a flat circle) and gently peel it away from the plastic. Lay the dough circle in a hot skillet sprayed with olive oil cooking spray. Repeat the process with each dough ball (tortilla)—use additional spray as necessary—spraying between dough balls if necessary. Clean or discard plastic bags when finished.

Huge Batch Chicken Stock for Recipes

This recipe has instructions for roasting the chicken first; if you want to save that step, just put the uncooked birds right into the stockpot—but the roasting gives it an awesome flavor!

Ingredients:
Olive oil cooking spray

6–8 pounds chicken (3 whole chickens), quartered, fat removed (keep all bones—use neck, heart, and gizzard—not the liver). *Note:* Remove breast meat after roasting and reserve for another recipe

3 large sweet yellow onions, peeled and quartered

1 bulb garlic, cloves separated and peeled

1 cup white wine

6 carrots, trimmed and peeled

1 whole celery heart, ribs trimmed and core discarded

1 2–3 inch piece of fresh ginger, peeled

Lemon verbena sprigs, or a 3-inch piece of lemongrass, or 1 Meyer lemon, halved

1–2 hot peppers (Thai or finger peppers), trimmed (seeded and deveined, if less heat is desired)

Fresh parsley sprigs

Fresh rosemary sprigs

Fresh thyme sprigs

Kosher or sea salt

20 cups cold water (or enough to cover ingredients)

Directions:
Preheat oven to 350°F. Place oven rack to middle position.

In a large roaster coated with olive oil cooking spray, add chicken, onions, and garlic (salt lightly if desired).

Place in oven and bake for about 35 minutes; splash with wine and continue to bake, basting periodically (total baking time will vary depending on size of pieces), until well cooked and nicely browned. Set aside to cool slightly.

In a huge stockpot, add roasted chicken and assorted bones (neck, etc.), add carrots, celery, ginger, lemon verbena or lemongrass, peppers, parsley, rosemary, and thyme.

Cover with water and place on stove over medium heat. When it comes to a boil, skim any foam from top and discard. Reduce heat to just a simmer and continue to cook for at least 6 hours. Add more water if necessary to keep all submerged. Adjust seasonings.

With a fine mesh strainer or colander lined with doubled cheesecloth and set in a huge bowl, ladle stock through the strainer; quickly cool and refrigerate (do not cover completely until stock chills thoroughly, e.g., overnight). Remove fat and discard (if fat is not removable with a spoon, lay paper toweling over stock and pat down slightly—toweling will absorb the fat). Once stock is cold, keep refrigerated or freeze in containers for later use. *Note:* You can keep stock refrigerated 4–5 days. Freeze 3–6 months (though closer to 3 is better).

Cooking Lobsters

Buy lobsters that are in tanks and are alive!! Make sure they are active. Bring them home and cook immediately or put them in the coldest area of the refrigerator. Make sure the lobsters are removed from the plastic bag they traveled in; an empty vegetable drawer works perfectly for short-term storage.

Directions:
When ready to cook (I remove the rubber bands from the lobster claws although you don't have to): In a large stockpot with lid, bring about 2–3 inches of cold water and a half lemon (or 2) to a rolling boil over medium-high heat. While waiting for the water to boil, stand the lobster on its head on a flat surface and rub the tail going downward – when the legs drop, you will notice the lobster appears to be asleep. Continuing to hold the lobster head down, plunge the head into the boiling water to kill it. Let go of the lobster and cover the pot; return to a boil. Cook about 18 minutes for a 1 1/4–1 1/2 pound lobster and 20–22 minutes for a 2–3 pound lobster.

Note: Some lobsters have hard shells, some soft. If a soft shell, reduce the cooking time by 2–3 minutes. When lobsters are fully cooked, they will turn bright red. Remove the lobster from the pot and drain.

Handling Fresh and Dried Morels: Storing, Preserving, and Reconstituting

If you talk to a dozen morel mushroom hunters, you will likely get a dozen opinions about handling, preserving, and reconstituting Morels (grays, blacks, and blondes). All chefs, mushroom hunters, and foodies alike have their own methods for these processes. After years of experience; I share with you, my "morel decisions."

Handling and Storing Fresh Morels

When handling morels after a spring/early summer foray, always collect them in a basket or bag made of mesh or one that has good air flow. Never collect them in a plastic bag or store them in one! Once you have arrived at your destination and are ready to prepare them (or want to keep them for later use), gently transfer them to an open basket, keep them in the mesh bag, or place them in a paper sack. Refrigerate your morels in a paper sack or paper towel-lined container, making sure no added moisture can infiltrate your prized finds. Refrigerated, they will last up to about a week—check for mold and any deterioration prior to use.

Preparing Fresh Morels for Cooking

As with any type of edible fungi, you want to find morels that are not old and bug eaten, broken, moldy, or larvae infested. When ready for cooking, cut off most of the stem (or all, in some cases, and save the stems for stock), and then lightly dust with a soft brush (check under description in the section "Reconstituting Dried Morels"). If there is a question of their cleanliness or bug infestation, cut them in half lengthwise—if keeping them whole (or the halves) you can lightly rinse them under cool water. Do not soak them as they will absorb more water than necessary, which will affect the overall flavor. Once drained, lightly pat dry with a clean cotton kitchen towel, being mindful not to break the patterned crevices of this prized mushroom. Make sure they are always cooked prior to consumption. If possible, cook prior to adding them into a recipe.

Preserving

Preserving can cover many aspects: fresh morels, cooked morels, and foods with morels contained within a recipe.

Preserving Fresh Morels

Drying: First and foremost, make sure they are clean and free of critters and debris. Bugs and worms are not uncommon to these fungi—morels have an abundance of crevices and crannies to hide in. There is a plethora of drying techniques available: oven drying at very low temperatures or gas ovens with the door ajar; drying out in sunlight on a nylon-mesh window screen; threading them using a needle and strong coat thread and stringing them up in an open uncluttered area until dry; or using commercially made dehydrators (following the manufacturers directions).

Regardless of drying method, make sure they are completely dry prior to storage. Store dried morels in airtight containers away from sunlight, heat, and moisture. Glass is always my preferred storage container.

Freezing: While some foragers swear by direct freezing, it is not my chosen method—morel mushrooms must be very clean and frozen quickly in airtight containers or plastic bags.

Because of the high moisture in mushrooms, I personally feel a great deal of the flavor is almost immediately lost in this process as well as a significant change in texture. If freezing in glass, make sure the glass containers used are freezer safe.

Packing in oil or vinegar: Usually referred to as pickling. Use safe canning methods and an oil or vinegar-type brine. The morels are blanched first and then canned. It is always essential to use fine quality oil or vinegar: much like cooking with wine, the better the product, the better the result. Be careful not to overflavor the brine or oil; what you want is the morel flavor to be entirely dominant. When you are ready to use them and you break the seal, store in the refrigerator, and use fairly quickly.

Packing in salt: If this is your chosen method, make sure to use a container that will not corrode from the use of salt (it is powerful): glass is always a safe bet. Morels are layered with salt, and proportions are 3 to 1 (3 being the morels).

Note: When ready to use the morels, remove as much salt as possible. For those watching their sodium intake, this is not a recommended method of preservation.

Preserving Cooked Morels

Sautéed: When morels are sautéed in olive oil, butter substitute, or liquid (reserved morel liquid, wine, or their own juice), they can then be successfully frozen for storage. Your final product will be ready for use in a recipe or as a topping. As with anything frozen, use an airtight container that is freezer safe or an ice cube tray (great for soups and sauces). When ready for use, it is best to use them directly from the freezer without defrosting.

In recipes: Morels in recipes freeze well; as a substantially structured, full-flavored mushroom, they have the ability to retain their texture and flavor throughout the freezing process. I always use freezer-safe glass containers with plastic lids (called working glass jars, they are available at some kitchen shops).

Reconstituting Dried Morels

I always begin the reconstituting process by lightly brushing my dried morels over a clean piece of paper. I use a soft baby hairbrush, natural bristle paintbrush, or a fluffy natural bristle cosmetic brush (one generally used for applying blush). Regardless of the specific brush I am using, I initially use a brand new clean brush and set it aside in a marked plastic bag "MORELS"—I never want that brush being used for any other purpose. It is kept solely for morels.

Why the clean paper below it? To catch any spores that may be released in the process. When done brushing the morels, I take the spore-spotted paper and shake it out in my wooded lot with the hope that new morels will appear the following year (wishful thinking!).

While you are busy brushing those masters of camouflage, boil about 4 to 6 cups of water and let it cool slightly. Place the brushed dried morels in an extra-large measuring cup or bowl and pour the previously boiled water over them. I usually set a ladle or kitchen tool on the top of the water to keep the morels submerged for 20 to 30 minutes to reconstitute. Once they are plumped, remove the morels from the water with a slotted spoon and retain the mushroom-infused liquid. The morel liquid is great for assisting in the sautéing of morels, used as part of a soup base, grain preparation, gravy base, or for additional recipes. I never just throw out the morel liquid. If ever there just too much to deal with, I freeze it in ice cube trays or throw it in areas where morels can potentially grow.

Ingredients that Marry Well with Morels

While many food-related "spring things" go well together, there are a lot of other ingredients that also pair well with the prized morel. Keep focused on the word *earthy*.

Ale
Bread, bread crumbs (panko)
Cider
Coconut milk
Cognac
Dairy: cream, (fat-free) half and half, milk, yogurt
Eggs
Fiddlehead ferns
Fish
Fruits: dried cherries, raisins
Garlic
Ginger
Grains: farro, quinoa, rice
Herbs: cilantro, chives, lemon grass, lemon thyme, mint, parsley, rosemary, tarragon
Lemon
Lentils

Meats: beef, bison, lamb, rabbit, veal
Mushrooms: domestic and wild
Oils: butter, margarine, olive oil
Onions: leeks, scallions, ramps (wild leeks), shallots, red, Vidalia
Pasta
Pastry/dough, savory
Ponzu sauce (citrus-flavored soy sauce)
Poultry: chicken, duck, turkey
Rum
Seafood: clams, crab, crayfish, mussels, scallops, shrimp
Soy sauce
Stocks: beef, chicken, seafood, veal
Tamarind
Vegetables: artichokes, asparagus, corn, pea pods, potatoes (all types), spinach, spring peas, tomatoes
Wine: red, white

Index of Ingredients

Agave nectar, 3, 18–19, 87, 125

Ale, dark, 33, 103, 118–19

Allspice, 60

Anchovies, 14, 116

Anchovy paste, 9

Antelope, 52, 98–99

Apple cider, 50

Apricot preserves, 24

Arctic char, 81

Artichokes, 7, 70–71

Asparagus, 40, 57, 74, 90, 121

Bacon, 56

Baharat Spice, 96, 127

Basil, 37, 45, 70, 75, 76, 87, 109, 116

Bay leaves, 17, 52, 127

Beans: black, 82; green, 116; pinto, 56; white, 38

Beef, 60, 62, 66, 68, 78, 79, 99

Beer, lime-flavored, 56

Bison, 36, 51, 60, 66, 68, 79

Blackberries, 80

Bok choy, 45

Breads: baguette, 28; crostini, 28; flatbread, 14; Italian, 72; raisin, 113

Bread crumbs, 21, 25, 75

Cabbage, 45, 59, 96, 106

Capers, 14

Cardamom, 8–9, 54, 60, 127

Carrot, 35, 36, 49, 52, 62–63, 66, 68, 96, 108, 130–31

Cauliflower, 35

Cayenne, 14, 20, 21, 22, 33, 41, 54–55, 60, 75, 110, 114

Celery, 25, 26, 36, 42, 52, 57, 58, 66, 113, 130–31

Cheese: brie, 7, 15; cheddar, 33, 83, 115; chèvre, 14, 27, 93, 94–95; colby, 115; Jarlsberg, 25; light, 67; light cream, 14, 25, 83; mozzarella, 70–71; Parmigiano–Reggiano, 28, 29, 51, 72, 76–77, 83, 109, 110, 112, 115; ricotta, 70–71, 105; Stilton, 22

Cheesecake, 25

Cherries, dried, 121

Chicken, 8–9, 45, 50, 54–55, 56, 84, 130

Chiles and peppers: "ancient," 57; finger, 36, 52, 130; hot green, 9; jalapeno, 82; red hot, 94; red Thai, 8, 9, 45, 130; sorrento, 56

Chili: oil, 12; powder, 55, sauce, 125

Chinese five-spice powder, 9, 50, 125

Chipotles, 59, 94–95, 116–17

Chives, 14, 26, 27, 33, 59, 78, 94, 97, 120

Cider, apple, 50; hard, 81

Cilantro, 24, 44, 45, 56, 59, 87

Cinnamon, 127

Clam juice, 58

Clams, 42

Cloves, 112, 127

Coconut milk, 9, 42, 44, 45, 67, 81, 87, 118

Cognac, 106

Coriander, 54, 87, 127

Corn, fresh, 37

Cornmeal, 92–93, 110

Crab, 16, 21, 29, 57, 74

Crab base, 74

Crawfish, 58

Crème de cassis, 80

Cumin, 9, 54, 56, 60, 87, 94, 127

Curry powder, 35

Panko, 17, 20, 24, 82

Paprika, 115, 127

Parsley, 12, 14, 15, 35, 36–37, 56, 58, 60, 68–69, 73, 86, 88–89, 93, 94, 98, 105, 108, 109, 113, 116, 130–31

Pasta: farfalle, 109; Japanese buckwheat noodles, 51; lasagna, 70; penne, 76–77; soba, 51

Pastry, 7, 16, 22, 68, 74, 106

Pâté, 27

Peanut butter, 8–9, 125

Pea pods, 12, 45, 78, 88–89, 121

Peas, 103

Pepitas, 112

Pepper, white, 17, 34, 54–55, 74, 81, 83, 87, 96, 110, 127

Peppercorns, black, 127

Pepper flakes, crushed red, 8

Peppers. *See under* Chiles and peppers

Phyllo dough, 74, 106

Ponzu, 9, 79, 104, 125, 126

Pork, 38–39, 78, 104, 120

Potatoes, 17, 33, 35, 42, 68–69, 105, 108, 114, 115

Pumpkin, 112

Quail eggs, 10

Quesadillas, 15

Quinoa, 114

Rabbit, 73

Ramps, 7, 21, 72, 74, 80, 86, 118–19, 120, 121

Red pepper flakes, 8, 76, 84

Red pepper hot sauce, 14, 25, 58

Rice: arborio, 112; brown, 78, 96–97, 103, 120; wild, 86

RMJ's Garlic Essence, 28, 81, 90, 105, 113, 126

Rosemary, 38–39, 50, 52–53, 66, 74, 79, 113, 130–31

Rum, spiced, 7, 74

Sage, 94, 103, 112, 113

Salmon, smoked, 27

Scallions, 12, 16, 18, 26, 27, 41, 44, 45, 49, 57, 67, 78, 88–89, 104, 114, 120, 126

Scallops, 86

Sesame seeds, 26, 88–89, 104, 121

Shallots, 20, 21, 22, 50, 73, 75, 81, 86, 103, 116, 119

Shrimp, dried, 87, 120; fresh, 12–13, 24, 26, 45, 87, 88–89

Smoked salmon, 27

Smoked trout, 17

Spinach, 22, 26, 38–39, 45, 56, 67, 92–93, 128

Squash, winter, 11 Shrimp: dried, 87, 120; fresh, 12–13, 24, 26, 45, 87, 88–89

Stock: beef, 33, 36–37, 68–69, 76, 98, 119; chicken, 34, 38–39, 40, 41, 44, 45, 50, 52–53, 56, 73, 80, 104, 109, 110, 112, 113, 130; clam, 42; seafood, 58; veal, 98; vegetable, 35, 37

Sweet red peppers, 57

Tabasco®, 14, 25, 58

Tapioca, 66

Tarragon, 10–11, 49, 58, 64, 81

Tea seed oil, 29

Thyme, 34, 98, 130–31

Tomatoes: canned, 36, 52, 54–55, 58, 66, 76, 96; fresh, 36, 56, 92–93, 98, 116–17; paste, 51, 76, 87, 98, 125; sun-dried, 128

Tortillas, corn, 59, 130; flour, 15

Triple Sec, 28

Trout: lake, 90; smoked, 17

Turbinado sugar, 3

Turkey, 75, 94

Turmeric, 54

Vindaloo spice, 54

Vinegar, 10, 24, 26, 59, 80, 125, 126

White pepper, 17, 34

Wild game. *See under* Game, wild

Wine: red, 53, 62–63, 66, 76, 79, 98–99; white, 20, 58, 80, 81, 84, 88–89, 112, 130

Yogurt, 35, 54, 57, 96–97, 125

Zinfandel, 79

Zucchini, 37

FIN

Text design and composition by Mary Sexton
Text fonts: Minion and Scala Sans
Display font: Delphin

Minion, inspired by classical, old style typefaces of
the late Renaissance, was designed by Robert Slimbach
and first released in 1990.
—Courtesy www.myfonts.com

Scala Sans was designed by Martin Majoor and published
by FontFont in 1990. The form is based on a humanist model
with influences from different style periods.
—Courtesy www.martinmajoor.com

Delphin, a beautiful roman typeface with strong calligraphic
leanings, was designed by Georg Trump between 1951 and 1955,
and released by the Weber type foundry in Germany.
—Courtesy www.myfonts.com